The Gigantic Book of Bible Fun

Standard®
PUBLISHING

Cincinnati, Ohio

Published by Standard Publishing, Cincinnati, Ohio
www.standardpub.com

Compilation Copyright © 2012 by Standard Publishing

#15830. Manufactured in Newburyport, Massachusetts, USA, December 2011.

Project editors: Lu Ann J. Nickelson, Rosemary Mitchell
Cover design: Dale Meyers
Interior Design: Sandra S. Wimmer
Production: Creative Services
Illustrators: Len Ebert, Dan Foote, Roy Green, Daniel Grossmann, Judy Hand, Matt
Key, Emilie Kong, Carl Moore, Nan Pollard, Jennifer Schneider, Janet Skiles,
Andy Stiles, Michael Streff, Raleigh Swanson

ISBN: 978-0-7847-3354-7

17 16 15 14 13 12   1 2 3 4 5 6 7 8 9

Creation Code

Use the code to find out two things God made in the beginning.

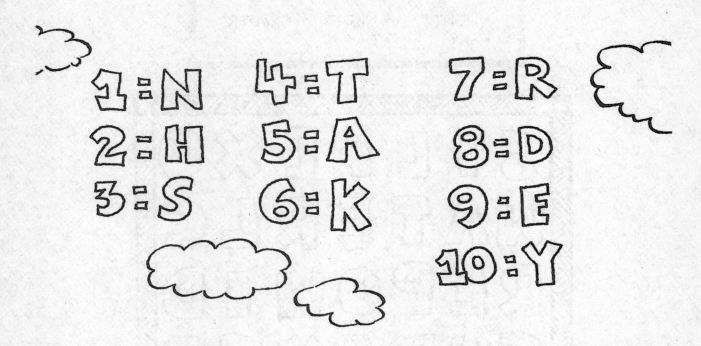

1:N   4:T   7:R
2:H   5:A   8:D
3:S   6:K   9:E
                10:Y

___ ___ ___   ___ ___ ___   ___ ___ ___ ___ ___
3 6 10   5 1 8   9 5 7 4 2

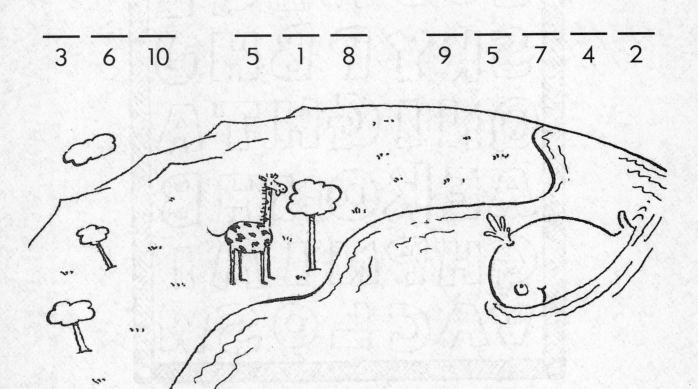

Find the Words

Find the five things God made on the first two days of creation. Look up, across, and down.

- LIGHT
- NIGHT
- WATER
- SKY
- DAY

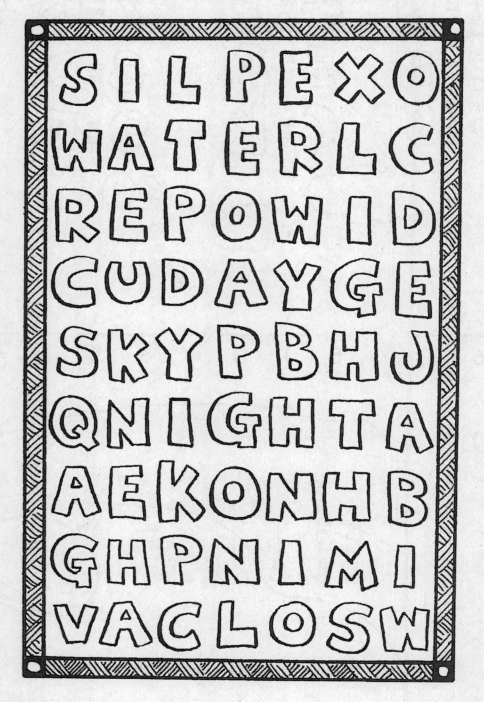

God Made

Connect the dots to discover some things God made.

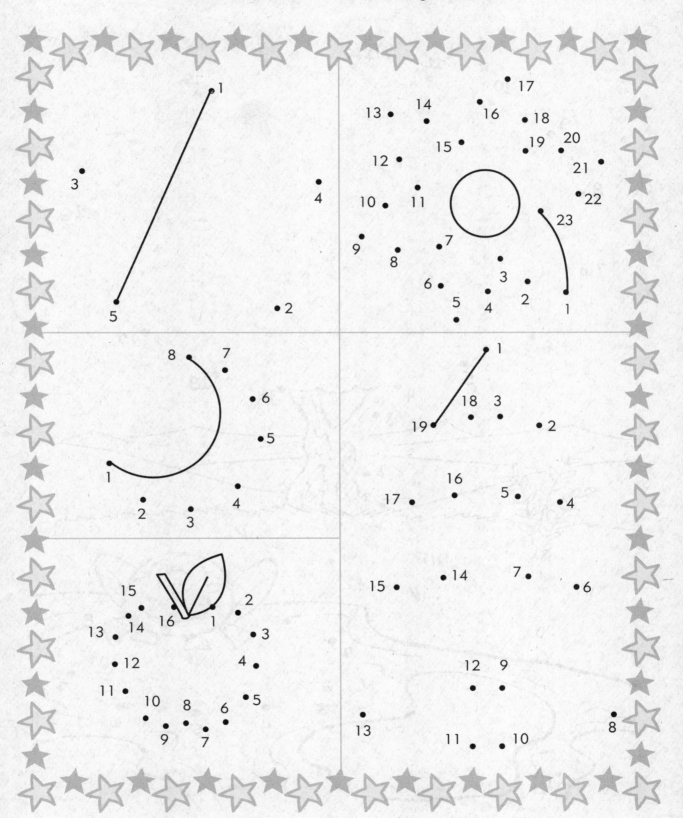

Connect the Dots

What did God make on the third day?

Genesis 1

Word Wheel Game

On the fourth day, God made the sun, moon, and _____. Use the first letter of each picture to spell out the answer.

$\underline{\quad}\ \underline{\quad}\ \underline{\quad}\ \underline{\quad}\ \underline{\quad}$
1 2 3 4 5

Finish the Picture

Fill the basket by drawing pictures of good food God makes for us.

Genesis 1

Favorite Foods

Connect the dots to find some foods God has given us. Then draw your favorite food in the box.

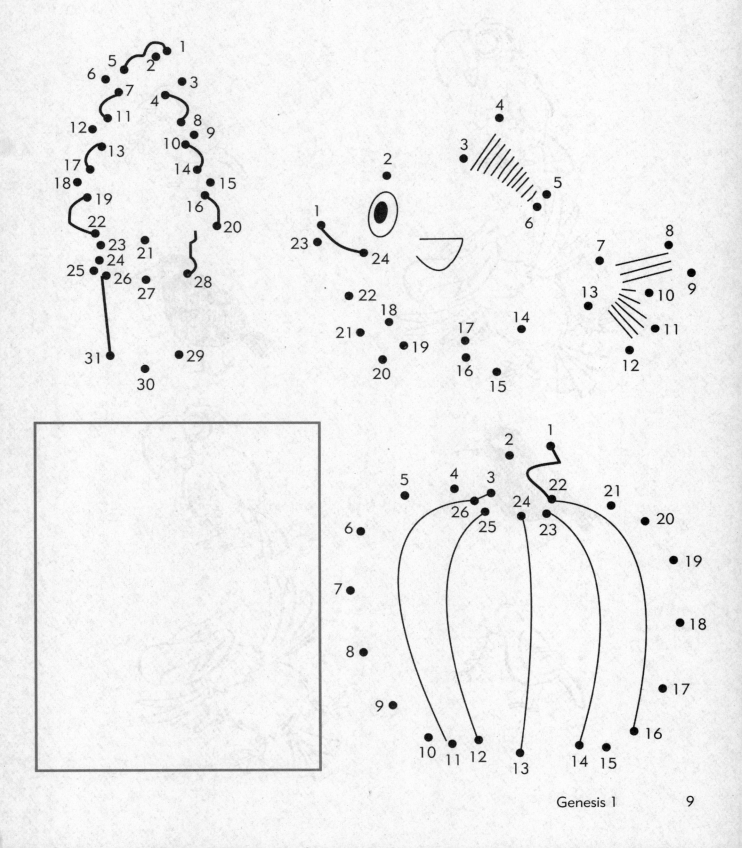

Feathered Friends

On the fifth day, God made all of the birds. Draw a line between the birds that are the same.

Swishy Fish

On the fifth day, God made all of the fish in the sea. Draw an X through each animal that is not a fish.

Animal Crossword

God made all of the land animals. Fill in the puzzle with the names of these animals.

What's Missing?

What makes these animals special? Finish each animal by drawing the missing part.

Finding Five

Five squirrels are hiding in this scene. Can you find them?

Find and Color

The lion is one of the mightiest animals that God created. Find the lion in the picture below by coloring the shapes with dots.

Follow the Dots

See what animal is taking a drink from the water.

God Makes the Animals

Color this picture of some of the animals God made.

Let There Be . . .

Starting with Day 1, find the correct path through the maze to the things that God created on that day. Do this until you have matched all the days with the correct pictures. Read Genesis 1:1-25 if you need help.

Find the Words

God made the world in six days and rested on the seventh. Find all these number words in the puzzle. Look up, down, and across.

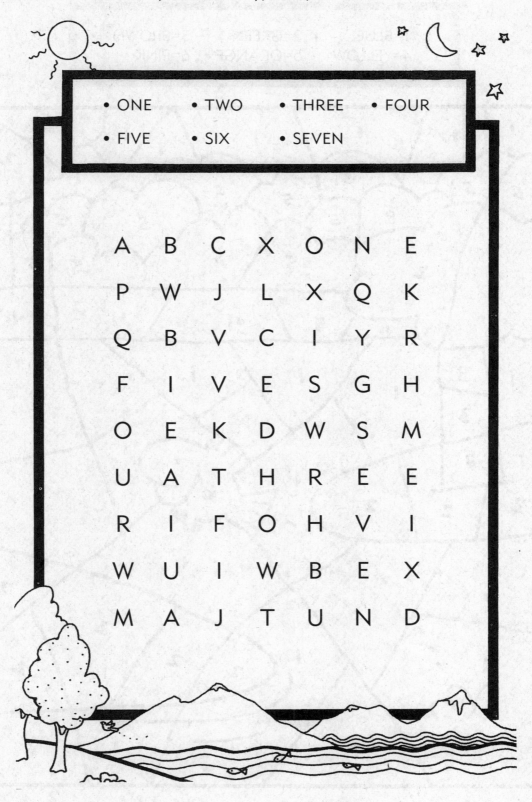

- ONE
- TWO
- THREE
- FOUR
- FIVE
- SIX
- SEVEN

```
A B C X O N E
P W J L X Q K
Q B V C I Y R
F I V E S G H
O E K D W S M
U A T H R E E
R I F O H V I
W U I W B E X
M A J T U N D
```

Color by Number

Use the code to color the Garden of Eden.

1=BLUE   2=GREEN   3=BROWN
4=YELLOW   5=ORANGE   6=PINK

Finish the Picture

Draw some of the things God made.

What's Wrong?

God created the first man, Adam. Find six things wrong with this picture.

Genesis 1, 2

Shadow Match

Match the picture of Adam with the correct shadow.

Do You See Them?

Adam named all the animals God made. Find five animals hidden in the picture.

Genesis 1, 2

Animal Unscramble

Why was Adam lonely? Write the word on each animal in the blank with the same number.

_____ _____ _____ _____ _____
   1   2   3   4   5

_____ _____ _____ _____ _____.
   6   7   8   9   10

Adam and Eve Maze

God created the first woman, Eve. Help Eve get through the maze to find the first man God created, Adam.

START

FINISH

Garden Maze

On the sixth day, God made Adam and Eve. Help Adam and Eve get to the river to get a drink.

Which One?

God told Adam and Eve to take care of the Garden of Eden. Which of these flowers in the garden is different?

Everything Was Good!

God said everything He made was good. The word *good* begins with the letter *g*. Circle everything in the picture that begins with the letter *g*.

Adam Riddle

What time did Adam leave the Garden of Eden? To answer the riddle, write the first letter of each picture clue.

Garden of Eden Riddle

After Adam and Eve left the Garden of Eden, why didn't the serpent argue its side of the story? To answer the riddle, write the first letter of each picture clue.

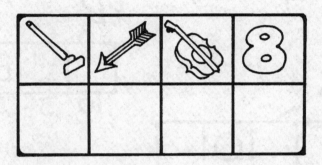

Genesis 1, 2   31

Adam and Eve Riddle

What did Adam and Eve do after they left the Garden of Eden? To answer the riddle, first write the names of the four picture clues. Then match the numbers to fill in the blank spaces below.

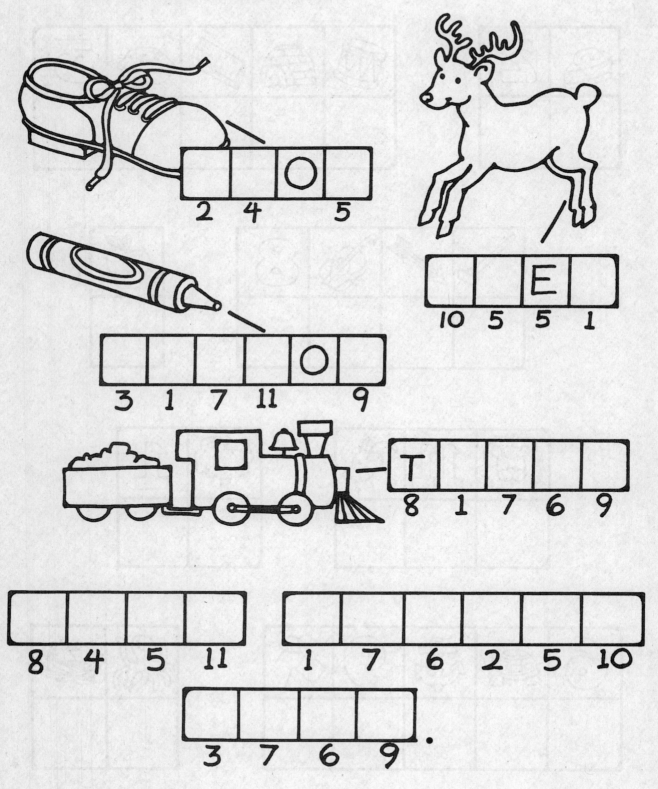

Build a Boat

God told Noah to build a big boat. Connect the dots to help Noah finish the ark.

Obeying God

God told Noah to build a very big boat for his family and two each of all the animals. Noah obeyed God. What happened next? Fill in the letter missing from each animal pictured. Copy the missing letters in order onto the lines at the bottom of the page. These letters will spell the answer. You can read about this in Genesis 6 and 7.

P I ☐

M O ☐ S E

☐ O L P H I N

☐ N A K E

B E ☐ R

A A R D ☐ A R K

T I G ☐ R

B I R ☐

L I O ☐

C ☐ W

C ☐ T

☐ O R S E

_ _ _

_ _ _ _ _

_ _ _ _ _ .

Animal Pair-Up

God told Noah to put pairs of every animal on the ark. Draw a line between the animals that are alike.

Looking for a Big Boat

Help the animals find their way to Noah's ark.

Genesis 6, 7

Slow Poke

Connect the dots to see the slowest animal on Noah's ark.

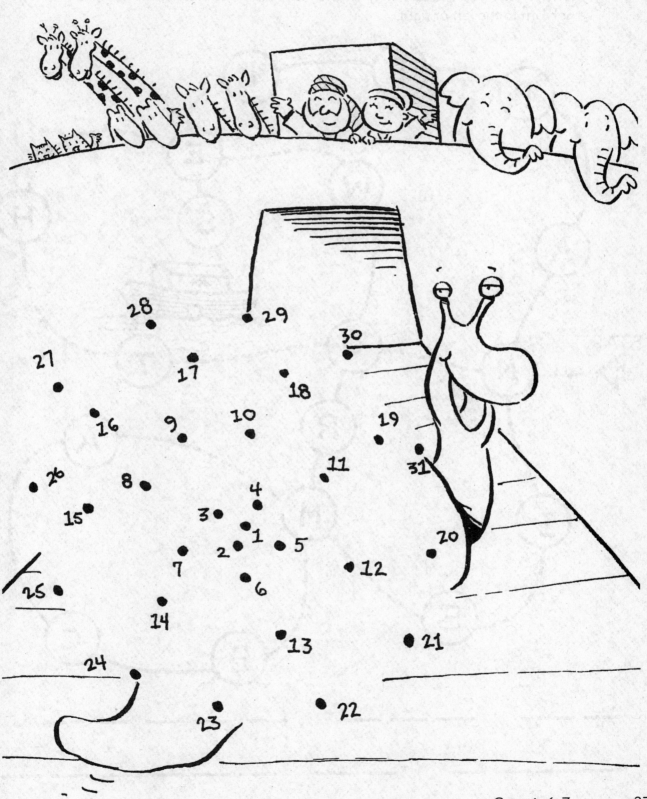

Ark Riddle

Did all the creatures come to the ark in pairs? To answer the riddle, start at the arrow and follow the path until you reach the ark. When you come to a letter, write it in a space below. Always move directly through each letter. Do not turn to the left or right.

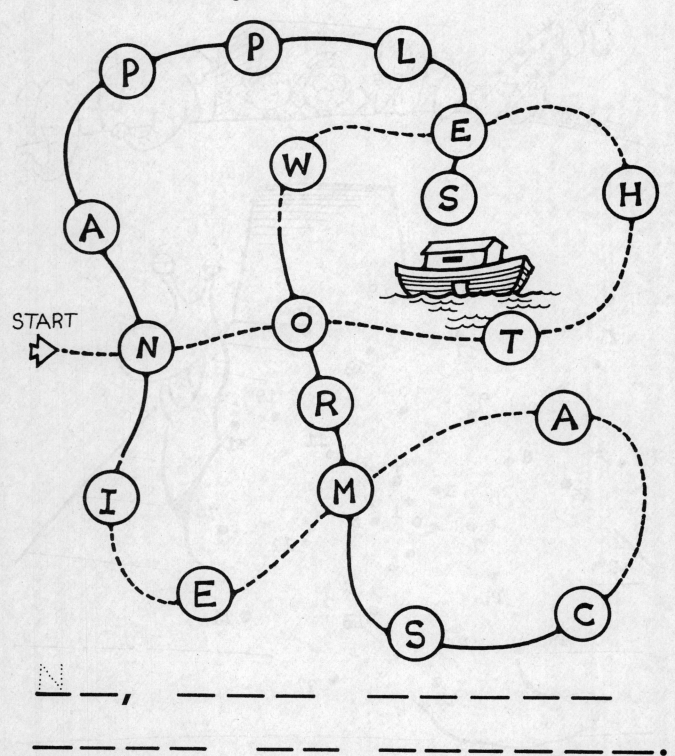

N __ __ , __ __ __ __ __ __

__ __ __ __ __ __ __ .

Do You Know?

God sent a lot of rain after Noah's family and all the animals were safely on the ark. Use the code to find out how long it rained.

1=Y   2=F   3=S   4=O   5=A   6=R   7=D   8=T

__ __ __ __ __   __ __ __ __
2 4 6 8 1   7 5 1 3

What's Wrong Here?

There are five things wrong with this picture. Can you find them all?

Genesis 6, 7

Noah and the Ark

Circle the things in the picture that Noah and his family could not do on the ark. Can you find all nine?

Finish the Picture

Use the dotted lines and the squares below to finish the other half of this hippo on Noah's ark.

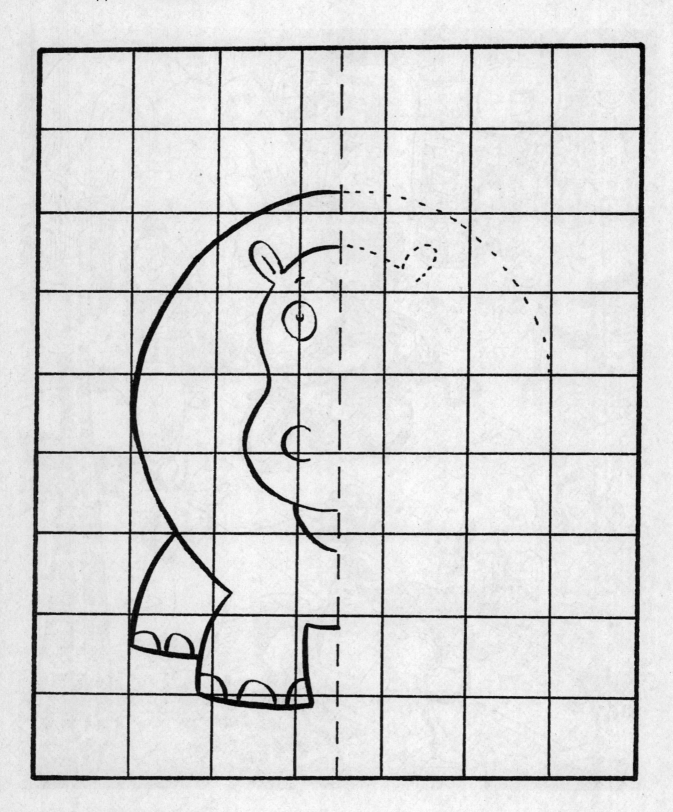

Genesis 6, 7

Word Search

Find the animal names in the puzzle below. Look up, across, and down.

T L D O G I B
U B O L C J T
D E V P R S U
P Y E J C X W
C H I C K E N
O L W M I A Y
W U X B P T L
A B C D E E R
P F O X W U T

Word Bank

- COW
- FOX
- DEER
- DOG
- CHICKEN
- DOVE

Funny Monkeys

Noah may have put vines in the ark so the monkeys could play. Only two of these monkeys are the same. Can you find them?

Match the Shape

After the rain stopped, Noah sent out a dove to look for dry land. Can you find this dove in the jumble of other animals below?

Noah Riddle

What did Noah use to light the ark at night? To answer the riddle, use the decoder to change each picture to a letter.

Maze

Help this dove get through the maze and back to Noah's ark.

Animals on Parade

Finally the ark came to rest on dry ground. Draw the animals coming out of the ark.

Color by Code

Use the color code below to color the rainbow God put in the sky.

B=BLUE   R=RED   G=GREEN
Y=YELLOW   O=ORANGE

Picture Match-Up

Abraham was the father of the Israelites, God's special people. Draw a line between the two pictures of Abraham that are the same.

Abraham's Journey

One day God spoke to Abraham. God told Abraham to leave his home and to go to Canaan to make a new home. Abraham did what God told him to do. Can you help Abraham find the way to the land of Canaan?

Lot Chooses

Lot moved with Abraham to a place called Bethel. They had so many flocks and herds that they needed to move apart. Abraham let Lot choose which way to go. Lot chose the plain cf Jordan. It had the best land and water. Abraham lived in Canaan. You can read about it in Genesis 13:5-12.

Begin at the center with Abraham and Lot. Find a path through the maze so that Lot arrives at the Jordan plain and Abraham arrives at Canaan.

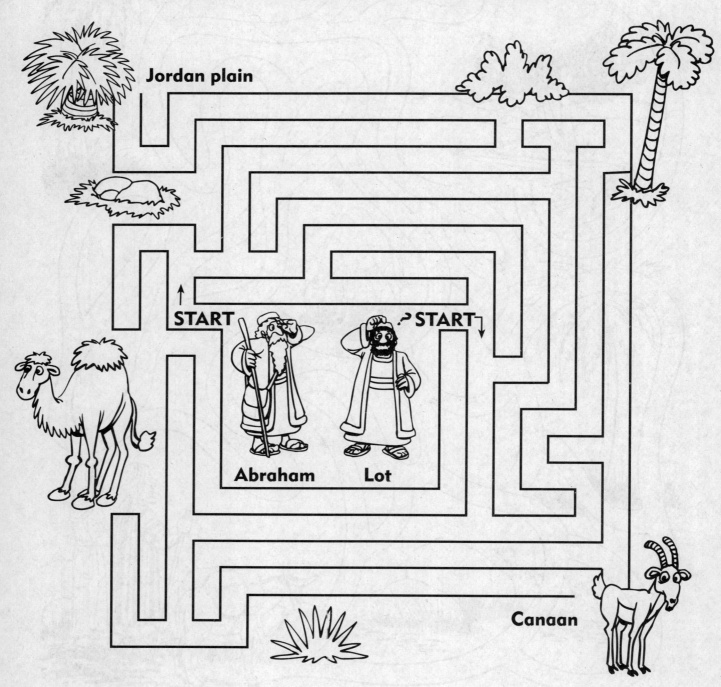

Jordan plain

START

START

Abraham

Lot

Canaan

Discover the Message

God sent visitors to tell Abraham that Sarah would have a son. Cross out the tents that are different. Then read what the visitors said.

A New Baby

Abraham and Sarah were very old when God let them have a baby. Do you know what they named this child? Color all the spaces with the letter *i* to find out. His name can be found in Genesis 21:1-7.

Picture Match-Up

God gave Sarah a baby when she was old. Draw a line between the two pictures that are alike.

Rebekah Is Kind

Color this picture of Rebekah showing kindness to Abraham's servant.

Isaac Is a Peacemaker

Isaac kept moving to keep peace because others wanted something that belonged to him. Use the code to find out what they wanted.

1=W	2=S	3=L	4=O	5=F
6=E	7=R	8=T	9=A	

__ __ __ __ __   __ __   __ __ __ __ __
1 6 3 3 2   4 5   1 9 8 6 7

Word Search

Isaac was an old man when he gave his blessing to Jacob. Find these four words in the puzzle below. Look up, down, across, and backwards.

• ISAAC   • JACOB   • BLESSING   • OLD

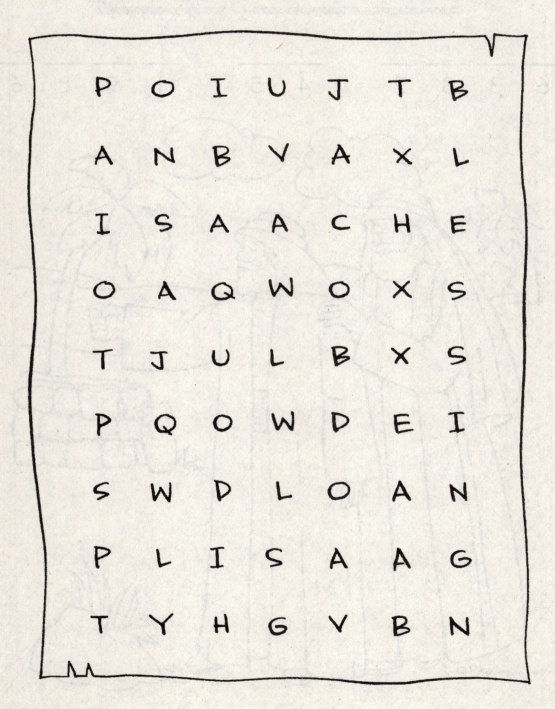

P O I U J T B
A N B V A X L
I S A A C H E
O A Q W O X S
T J U L B X S
P Q O W D E I
S W D L O A N
P L I S A A G
T Y H G V B N

Color by Number

Color the picture of Jacob's dream.

1=YELLOW	2=PURPLE	3=BROWN
4=WHITE	5=GREEN	6=BLUE

God Cares for Jacob

Finish this picture of Jacob's dream by drawing angels on the stairway.

Genesis 28

God Cares for You

Think about how God cared for Jacob. Then think about how God cares for you. Use the picture clues and the Word Bank to do the puzzle.

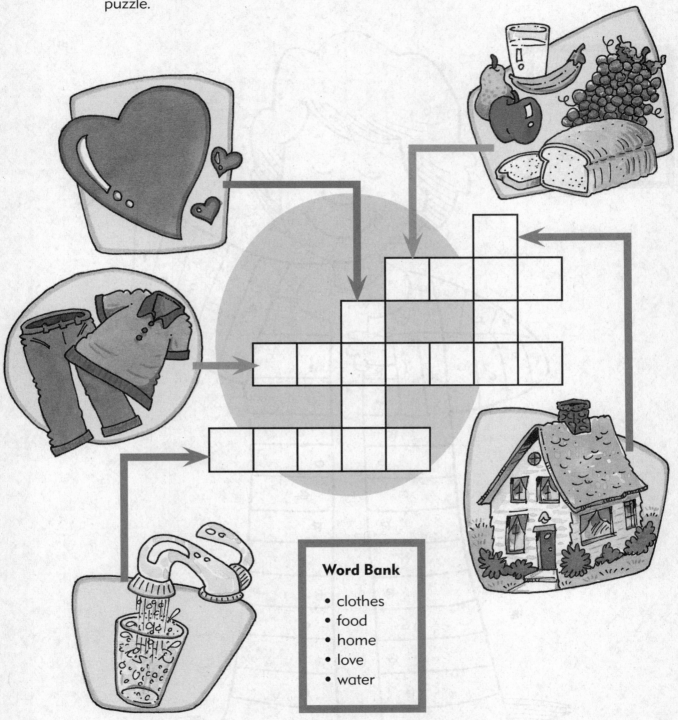

Word Bank

- clothes
- food
- home
- love
- water

Color Code

Joseph's father gave him a coat of many colors. Maybe it looked like this. Use the code to color the coat.

R=RED
Y=YELLOW
B=BLUE
G=GREEN
O=ORANGE

Missing Pieces

Joseph's jealous brothers sold him to traders who took him to Egypt. Place the puzzle pieces into the puzzle.

God Helps Joseph

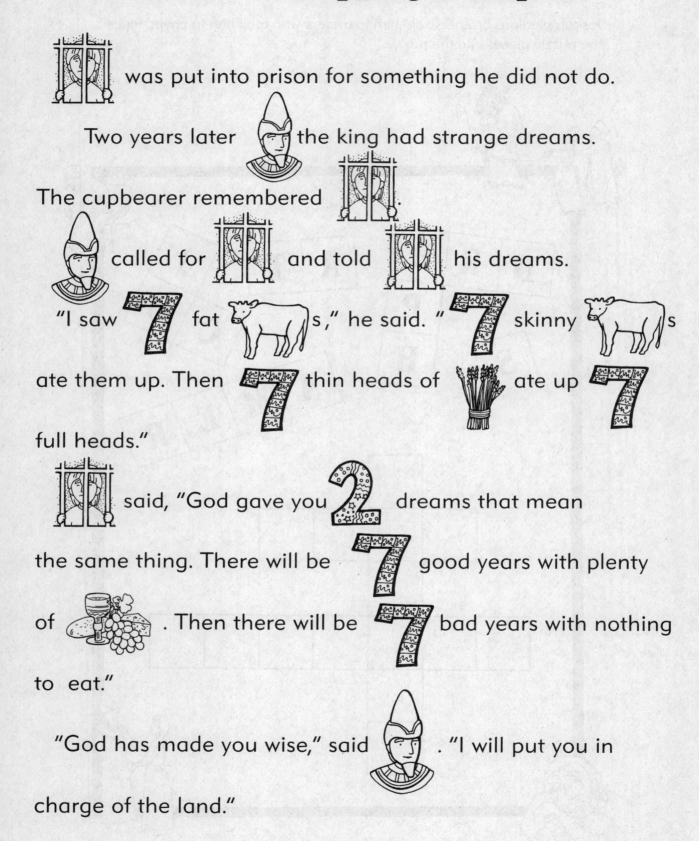

[Joseph] was put into prison for something he did not do.

Two years later [the king] the king had strange dreams.

The cupbearer remembered [Joseph].

[The king] called for [Joseph] and told [Joseph] his dreams.

"I saw 7 fat [cow]s," he said. "7 skinny [cow]s ate them up. Then 7 thin heads of [grain] ate up 7 full heads."

[Joseph] said, "God gave you 2 dreams that mean the same thing. There will be 7 good years with plenty of [food] . Then there will be 7 bad years with nothing to eat."

"God has made you wise," said [the king] . "I will put you in charge of the land."

Who Was It?

Who put Joseph in charge of the land of Egypt? Write the first letter of the name of each picture.

$$\frac{}{1} \ \frac{}{7} \ \frac{}{3} \ \frac{}{4} \ \frac{}{6} \ \frac{}{3} \ \frac{}{2}$$

Joseph Riddle

Why did Pharaoh make Joseph a ruler? To answer this riddle, change each letter to the one that comes before it in the alphabet.

G	P	S

H	P	P	E

N	F	B	T	V	S	F

What's Wrong Here?

For seven years, crops did not grow. People came to Joseph to buy grain.
Find six silly things in this picture and circle them.

Number Code

God gave Joseph an important job. Use the code to find out how Joseph did his job.

$\overline{}\ \overline{}$ $\overline{}\ \overline{}\ \overline{}$ $\overline{}\ \overline{}\ \overline{}$ $\overline{}\ \overline{}\ \overline{}\ \overline{}$.

  4   1   2   3   2   4   3   5   7   1   5   6

5=S
1=E
3=I
4=H
7=B
2=D
6=T

Joseph Forgives

Color this picture that shows Joseph forgiving his brothers for the wrong things they had done to him.

Genesis 45   69

Connect the Dots

What was baby Moses' hiding place?

Moses' Hiding Place

How did God keep baby Moses safe? Color the spaces using the color code. Then write your answer on the line below.

1=RED   2=BLUE   3=BLACK   4=GREEN   5=BROWN

Mystery Maze

Where is the sound of crying coming from? Help the princess get through the reeds to baby Moses.

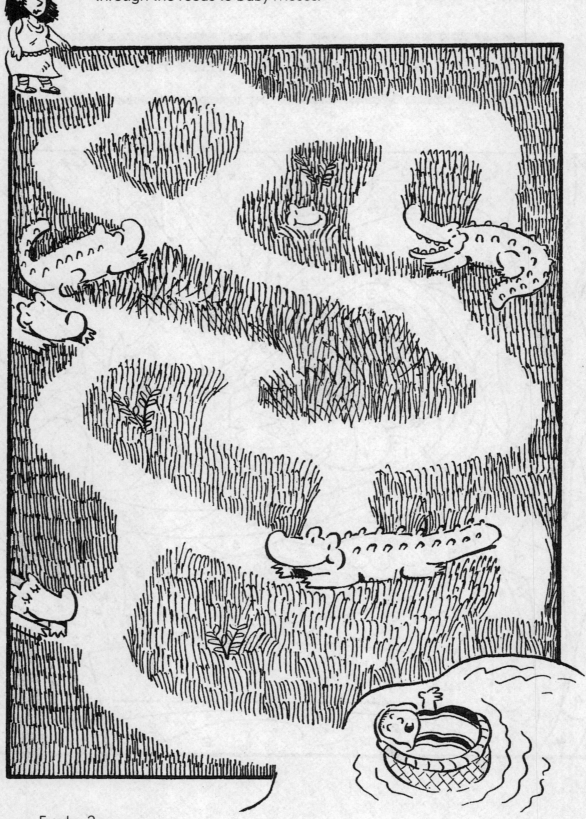

Water Baby

One day, when Pharaoh's daughter went to the river, she saw a basket in the tall grass. In the basket was a baby boy. Because the Hebrew baby boys were in danger, she guessed that this baby was a Hebrew. She felt sorry for him and decided to take him home and care for him. She gave him a very special name. Read about this in Exodus 2.

Use the code to find his name.

Use the code again to find out what his name means.

__ __ __ __ __ __ __

__ __ __ __ __ __ __ __

What's Wrong?

Pharaoh's daughter found baby Moses floating in a basket. Find five things wrong with this picture.

Which One?

The princess asked Moses' mother to take care of him until he was old enough to live at the palace. Find the baby that is different from all the others.

Crossword

Fill in the crossword with the answers to the clues. Use the Word Bank for help.

Word Bank

- baby
- mother
- basket
- Nile
- king's
- sister
- Moses
- tar

Across

2. The baby's mother put him in a _____.

6. The king's daughter named the baby _____.

8. While the baby was in the river, his _____ watched him.

Down

1. The _____ was crying, and the king's daughter felt sorry for him.

3. The _____ daughter raised the baby as her son.

4. The basket was coated with _____ and pitch.

5. The baby's own _____ cared for the baby.

7. The baby's mother placed the basket along the banks of the _____ River.

What's Wrong Here?

Moses grew up in the palace of the king of Egypt. Find five things that are wrong in this picture.

Picture Search

Moses saw that his people, the Hebrews, had to work very hard in Egypt. Find these tools in the box in the same order as below. Look up, down, and across.

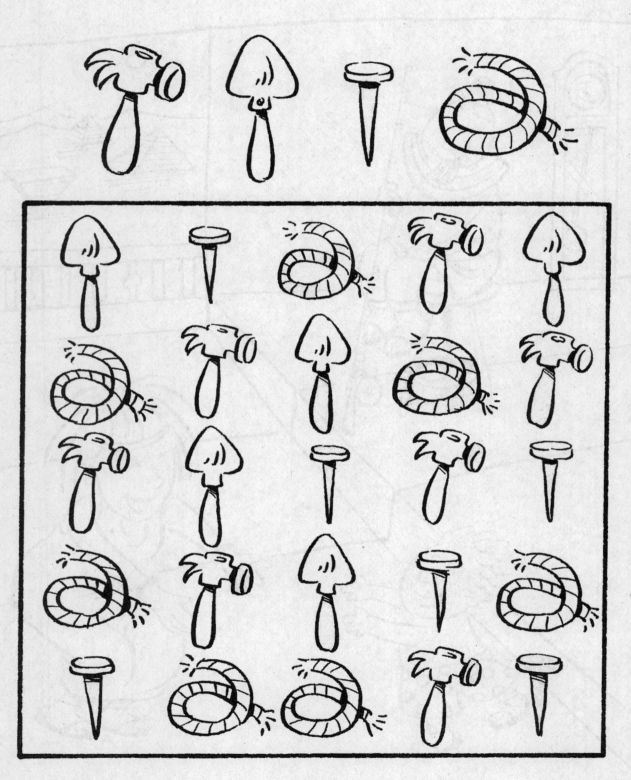

Color by Number

In the desert, God spoke to Moses from a burning bush. Color this picture using the color code.

1=BROWN   2=GREEN   3=BLUE
4=YELLOW   5=RED   6=TAN

The Burning Bush

Draw the burning bush from which God spoke to Moses.

Which One?

God talked to Moses from a burning bush that didn't burn up! Find the bush that is different.

Unscramble the Message

What did God tell Moses to do?

———— ———— ————
NRIGB   YM   OPLEEP

———— ———— ————
UOT   FO   YGPET.

Word Search

God told Moses to lead the Israelites out of Egypt. "I will be with you," God said. Find God's words in this puzzle. Look up, across, and down.

I WILL BE WITH YOU

```
D X M T W F L
W Q R C A R Z
I P Q W I O X
L Q H R Y O U
L Z T F G M E
G E I T T B E
V R W F D I M
H X G E S L N
Y G B K G R N
```

Desert Daze

Moses and his brother Aaron went to Egypt. Help them find their way through the desert.

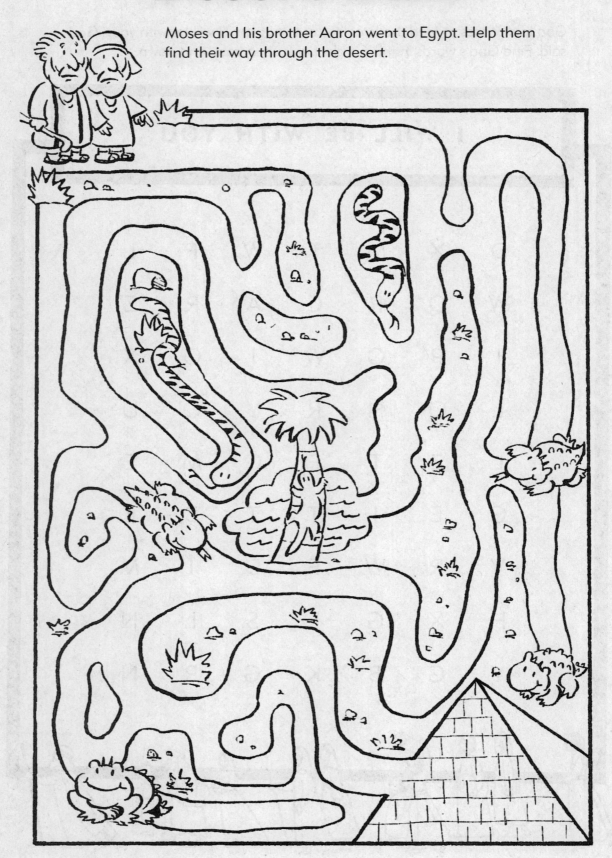

Find the Snakes

God changed Aaron's staff into a snake. Find the five snakes hidden in this picture.

Plaguing Problems

When Moses grew up, he was chosen by God to lead the Hebrews out of slavery. God sent plagues to the land of Egypt to help Moses convince Pharaoh to free the people. You can read about it in Exodus 7–14. Look for the ten plagues in this pyramid. They are hidden forwards, backwards, up, down, and diagonally.

```
K  B  O  I  L  S  T  S  L
N  C  O  B  G  X  S  I  B
S  A  O  U  E  E  A  S  L
E  N  E  T  N  H  X  G  O
I  S  K  K  S  J  I  O  O
L  T  R  M  C  E  P  R  D
F  A  L  B  V  C  V  F  F
D  N  H  T  A  E  D  I  Y
S  G  T  S  U  C  O  L  L
```

PLAGUES

BLOOD
FROGS
GNATS
FLIES
LIVESTOCK
BOILS
HAIL
LOCUST
DARKNESS
DEATH

Count the Frogs

God filled the land of Egypt with frogs. How many frogs can you find in this picture?

Help Them Out!

Can you help Moses lead the people out of Egypt without being affected by one of the plagues? To do it, you'll have to travel in and around the plagues without passing the openings of the circles. You must not leave the sand.

Draw and Color

During the daytime, God led Moses and the Israelites with a giant pillar of cloud. Draw the pillar of cloud. Then color the picture.

God Cares

Use the picture clues and the Word Bank to do the crossword puzzle.
Discover how God cared for Moses and the Israelite people.

Word Bank

- Moses
- fire
- desert
- night
- cloud
- day
- slaves

Where Was It?

Moses led God's people out of Egypt. Write the first letter of each picture to spell the name of the body of water they had to cross.

$\overline{}\ \overline{}\ \overline{}\quad \overline{}\ \overline{}\ \overline{}$
1　2　3　　4　5　6

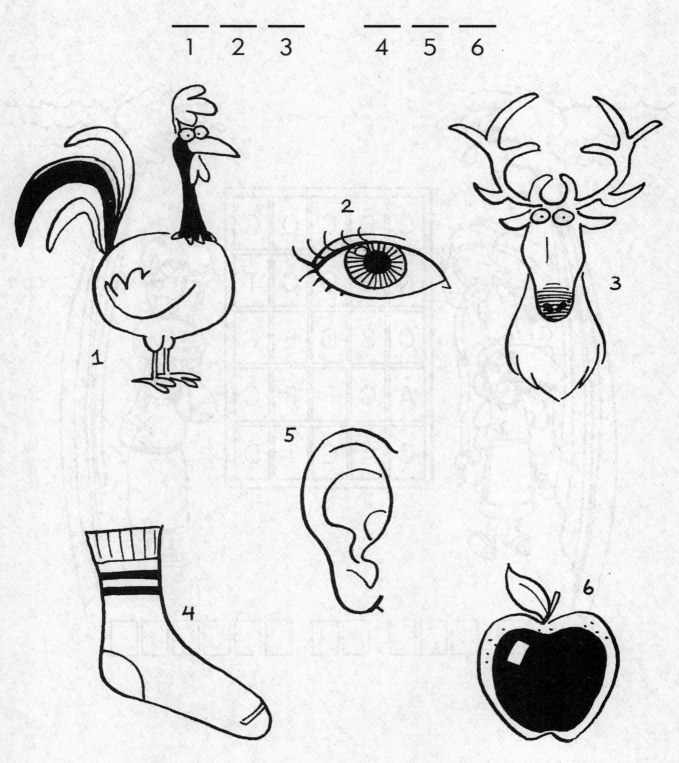

Red C, Red Sea!

Use a red crayon or marker to color every box containing the letter *C*. Transfer the leftover letters in order, row by row, to the spaces below to find out what Moses told God's people when it was time for them to cross the Red Sea. You can read the answer in Exodus 14:13.

C	D	C	O	C
N	C	O	C	T
C	B	C	E	C
A	C	F	R	C
C	A	C	I	D

☐☐ ☐☐☐ ☐☐ ☐☐☐☐☐☐ .

Color the Picture

God parted the Red Sea so Moses and the Israelites could escape from the Egyptians.

Crossing the Red Sea

Finish this picture by drawing the walls of water on each side of the Israelites.

Escape from Egypt

God took care of the Israelites. He parted the Red Sea so they could escape from the Egyptians. Circle these words in the word search below. Look across and down.

Word Bank

- PHARAOH
- HORSES
- GOD
- WIND
- CLOUD

- EGYPT
- MOSES
- RED SEA
- DRY

- CHARIOTS
- ISRAEL
- FIRE
- BELIEVE

```
P H A R A O H A C
D E G Y P T E F B
H I C L O U D J E
D L H O R S E S L
R N A O W I N D I
Y Q R R S T R U E
W X I S R A E L V
Z G O D W X D Y E
A B T C D E S F H
M O S E S I E J L
M F I R E N A O Q
```

Red Sea Riddle #1

How did the Red Sea greet the Egyptians when they tried to cross it? To answer the riddle, use a pencil to fill in every space that contains a dot.

Red Sea Riddle #2

Why was the Red Sea like a boy's head of hair? To answer the riddle, first find each of the two numbers that are alike. Then draw a line between them. Next, hold this page up to a mirror to read it.

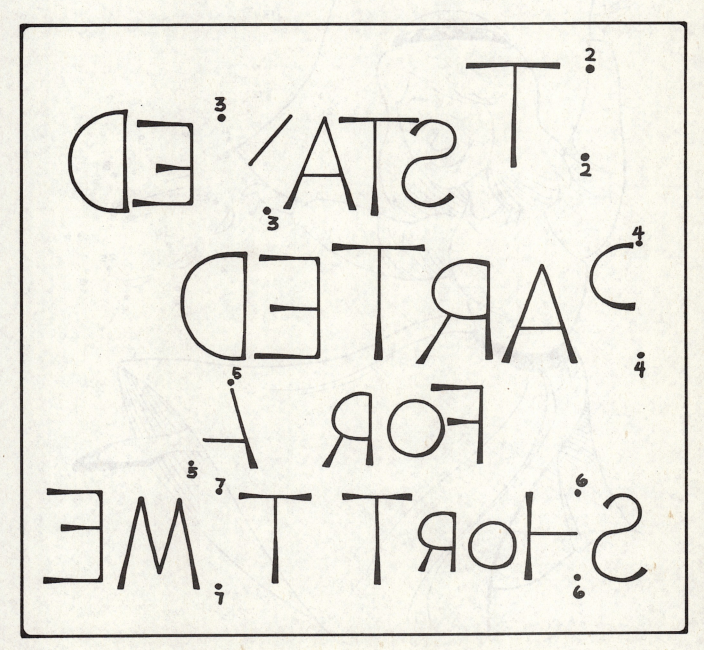

Connect the Dots

Moses' sister Miriam led the Hebrew women in a song. Connect the dots to see what instrument she played.

Picture Crossword

When and what did God give Moses and the Israelites in the wilderness?
Write the words in the correct puzzle space.

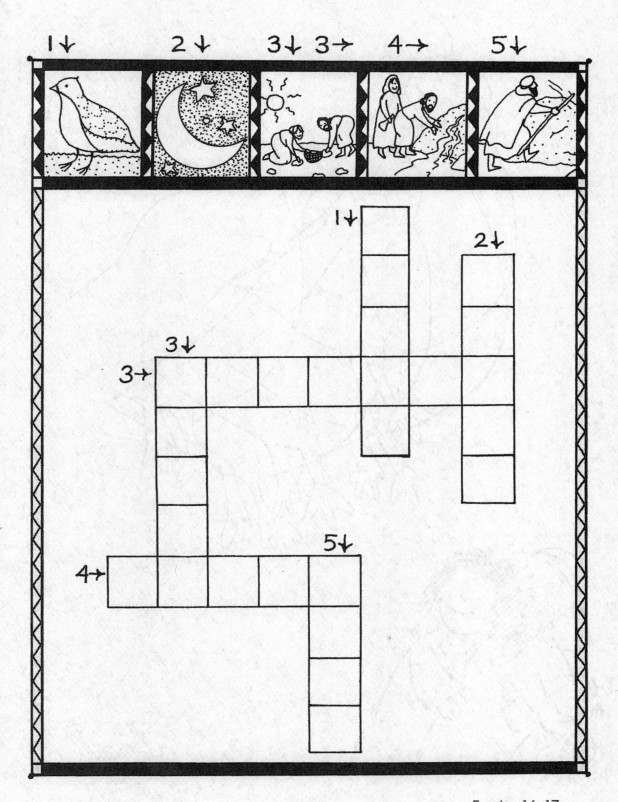

Count the Quail

In the wilderness, God sent quail for the Israelites to eat. How many quail do you see?

Find Six

God made water come out of a rock for the Israelites to drink.
How many things don't belong in this picture?

Moses on the Mountain

Help Moses climb the mountain where God gave him the Ten Commandments.

Moses Match-Up

God gave Moses the Ten Commandments on two stone tablets. Match the picture to the correct shadow.

God Gives Ten Rules

Color this picture of Moses holding the Ten Commandments.

Connect the Dots

God gave Moses the Ten Commandments. What did God write them on?

Believe God

When all the other Israelites were grumbling, two men said, "Do not rebel against the LORD! And do not be afraid of the people of the land" (Numbers 14:9). To find out who those men were, color the boxes containing the letters of the words in each row. The first row is done for you. The names of two brave men will appear in the uncolored boxes. Read each column from top to bottom. You can read all about them in Numbers 14:1-9.

DO NOT
REBEL
AGAINST
THE
LORD
DO NOT
BE
AFRAID

O	T	D	O	N	O	C	T
R	R	E	B	J	E	A	L
A	G	A	I	O	N	S	T
H	E	T	T	S	H	L	E
R	O	L	O	H	R	E	D
O	D	O	N	U	O	B	T
E	B	B	E	A	B	E	E
D	F	A	F	R	A	I	D

Do You Know?

Unscramble these words to see how old Moses lived to be.

_____ _____ _____ _____
NEO DHDUENR NDA NTYWTE

Joshua's Answer

When it was time for Moses to die, God told Joshua to lead his people, to be strong and brave, and to tell the people to obey and follow him with courage. Did Joshua obey God's commands? To find out, use a pencil to fill in every face that isn't smiling. When you're finished, you'll be able to see if Joshua obeyed God. You can read about this in Deuteronomy 31 and 34 and Joshua 1.

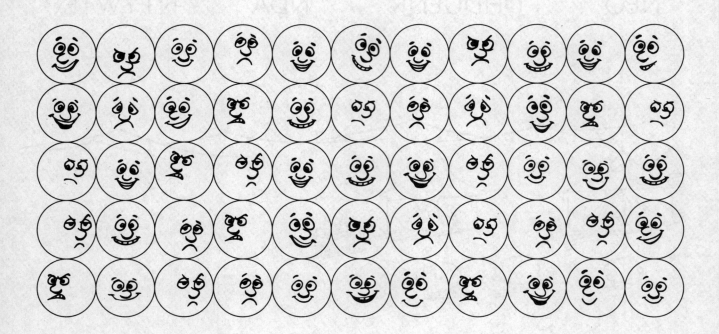

What should your answer be when God asks you to do something?

_____ _____ _____!

Joshua's Challenge

Start with the circled letter *B*. Circle every other letter. Continue all the way around the page. Then write the circled letters in order on the lines below.

Start Ⓑ m e e s a t l r t o v n y g o H w a r

B _ _ _ _ _ _ _ _ _ .

_ _ _ _ _ _ _ _ _ _ _ .

_ _ _ _ _ _ _ _ _ _ _ .

_ _ _ _ _ _ _ _ _ .

_ _ _ _ _ _ _ _ _ _ _ .

(Joshua 1:9)

Where Did They Go?

Rahab hid two Israelite spies and kept them safe. Use the code to find out where the men hid. You can check your answer in Joshua 2:4-6.

1=O	2=N	3=R	4=A
5=H	6=B	7=S	8=F

$\underline{}_1 \ \underline{}_2 \quad \underline{}_3 \ \underline{}_4 \ \underline{}_5 \ \underline{}_4 \ \underline{}_6 \ '\underline{}_7$

$\underline{}_3 \ \underline{}_1 \ \underline{}_1 \ \underline{}_8$

Joshua and Jericho

Fill in the crossword with answers to the clues. Use the Word Bank for help.

Across

4. The _____ fell on the seventh day.
8. God's people marched around _____.
9. Joshua told the people to _____ around Jericho.
10. Some priests blew on _____.

Down

1. The walls fell by the _____ of God

2. Joshua said, "Do not shout until I _____ you to."
3. The _____ walked behind the first group of priests.
5. The people marched around Jericho _____ days.
6. _____ was the leader of God's people.
7. God's people were told to _____ after the trumpet blast.

Word Bank

- trumpets
- walls
- Jericho
- tell
- Joshua
- power
- march
- seven
- shout
- soldiers

Connect the Dots

God helped Joshua defeat the city of Jericho. What fell down when Joshua's army obeyed God?

Find and Color

God told the people to march around Jericho seven times. Find and color seven trumpets.

The Walls of Jericho

God told the Israelites to march around the walls of Jericho for six days. On the seventh day they were to march around seven times. The priests blew on their trumpets, the people shouted, and the walls of the city fell. Here are three trumpet players. At first glance they all look the same. One, however, is different. Draw some lines to make him the same.

Here are three soldiers. See if you can make the different one match the others.

Make these three Israelite men match.

Word Search

Deborah was the first woman to lead God's people. Find these words that describe Deborah. Look across and down.

• LEADER   • PROPHET   • JUDGE   • BRAVE

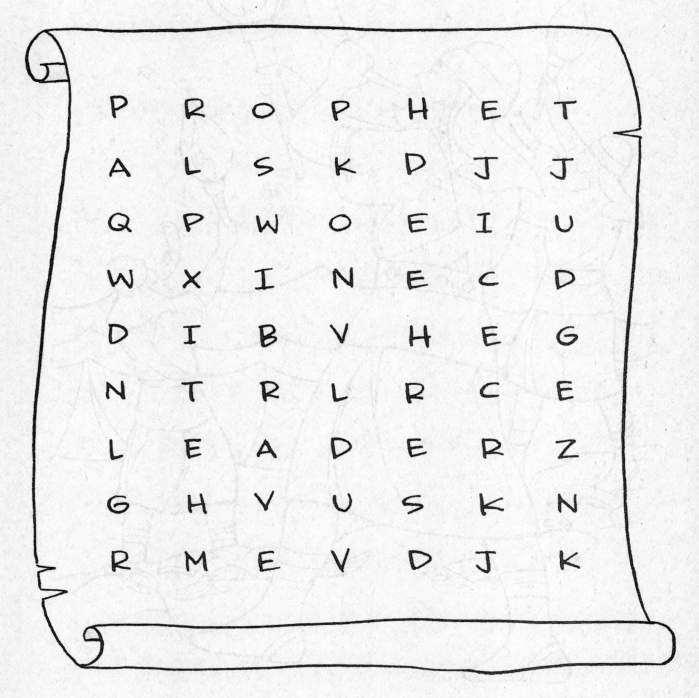

```
P  R  O  P  H  E  T
A  L  S  K  D  J  J
Q  P  W  O  E  I  U
W  X  I  N  E  C  D
D  I  B  V  H  E  G
N  T  R  L  R  C  E
L  E  A  D  E  R  Z
G  H  V  U  S  K  N
R  M  E  V  D  J  K
```

Gideon Is Brave

Color this picture of Gideon leading the Israelites into battle.

Samson Match-Up

God made Samson very strong. Circle the two pictures of Samson that are exactly alike.

Samson Riddle

What person in the Bible was most like an actor? To answer the riddle, write an *S* in each circle, an *O* in each square, and an *E* in each diamond.

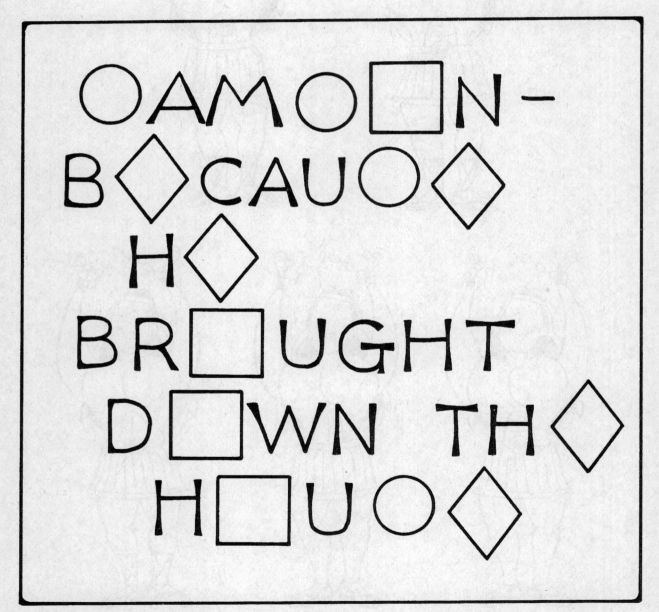

○AMO□N-
B◇CAUO○◇
H◇
BR□UGHT
D□WN TH◇
H□UO◇

Color and Find

Who was King David's great grandmother? Color the spaces that have dots.

Ruth Rebus

Color the pictures in the rebus. Use the rebus to retell the story of Ruth working hard in the fields to provide for herself and Naomi.

 Ruth Naomi home food fields grain Boaz

 was married to 's son. 's husband and 's husband died. decided to stay with .  took to Bethlehem to her in Judah. was sad. and did not have much . offered to go work in the gathering . collected the other workers left behind. owned the and was kind to . let pick from his as often as she wanted to. and had plenty of . worked in the every day from morning until night.

Number Code

Ruth was a great friend to her mother-in-law, Naomi. Use the code to find out what the name *Ruth* means.

1=D   2=F   3=I   4=R   5=E   6=N

$\overline{}$ $\overline{}$ $\overline{}$ $\overline{}$ $\overline{}$ $\overline{}$
2   4   3   5   6   1

Connect the Dots

Ruth was a good friend to Naomi. What did Naomi bake with the grain Ruth brought her?

Finish the Picture

Connect the dots to see what Hannah made for Samuel every year.

Sleepy Samuel

Write the *S* on the first blank. Cross out the next two letters. Write the next letter on the next blank. Keep going until you find out what Samuel did.

S B L A G I M T I U F Y E V N L P F L P D I Q

V S X B T L G E R J N D S E M F D W B T V H

O X U G Z J O Z W D Q R A K C N Y H D Q M

O E U B K J E C S Y N Z E T A D

S A M U E L   L I S T E N E D

T O   G O D   A N D   O B E Y E D.

Samuel Listened to God

Where was Samuel when he heard God's voice? Connect the dots to find out.

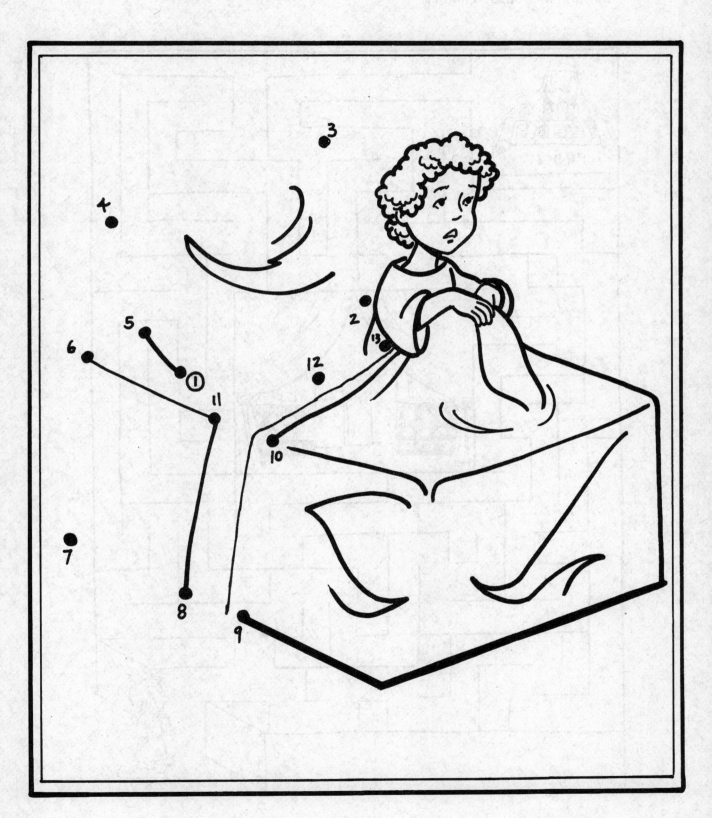

Maze

Samuel lived with Eli and helped him care for the temple. Lead Samuel through the maze to find Eli.

FINISH

START

1 Samuel 2, 3

Obey God

King Saul was a good king as long as he listened to God and did what God said. But when Saul decided to stop listening to God, he got into big trouble. God's prophet Samuel came to Saul and gave him some good advice.

You will get out of the maze only by following good advice. See what happens if you follow bad advice. You can find out how Saul disobeyed and what happened in 1 Samuel 15.

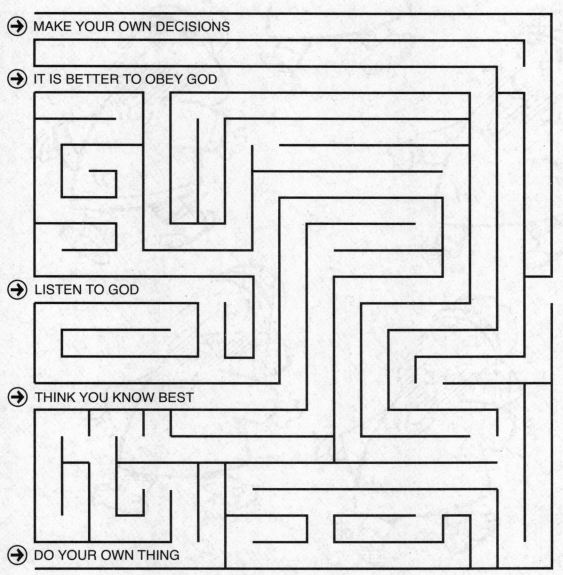

MAKE YOUR OWN DECISIONS

IT IS BETTER TO OBEY GOD

LISTEN TO GOD

THINK YOU KNOW BEST

DO YOUR OWN THING

Samuel Match-Up

The prophet Samuel said that David would one day become king of Israel.
Which two pictures of Samuel are exactly alike?

David Does His Job

David took care of sheep when he was young. Finish this picture by drawing the sheep David is protecting from the bear.

Connect the Dots

What kind of animal did David fight to protect his sheep?

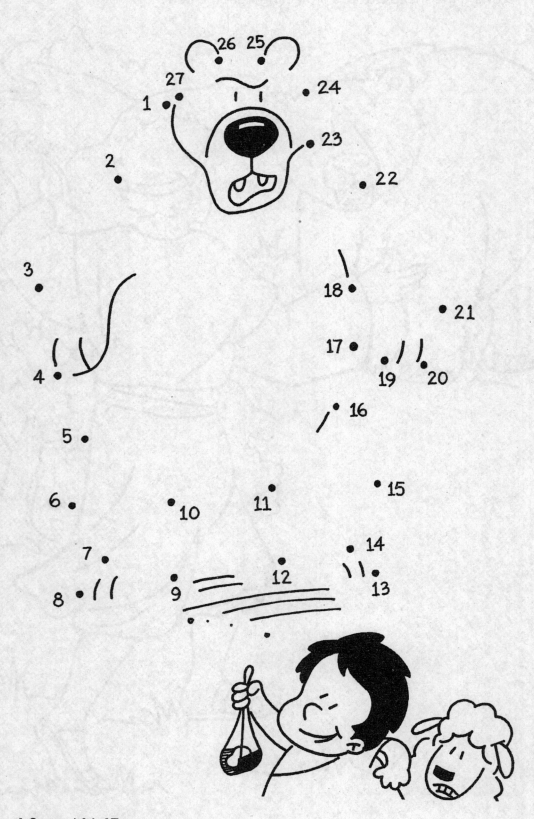

1 Samuel 16, 17

Find David's Lost Sheep

When David was young, he was a shepherd. Help David find his lost lamb.

How Many Brothers?

Hidden in the puzzle is the number of brothers David had. Find the number and color it.

Connect the Dots

What instrument did David play?

What's Wrong?

David often played his harp for King Saul. Circle the six things that are wrong in this picture.

1 Samuel 16, 17

Word Wheel

King Saul asked David to come to the palace to play his harp. Saul did not know that someday David would be the _____. Use the first letter of each picture to spell the answer below.

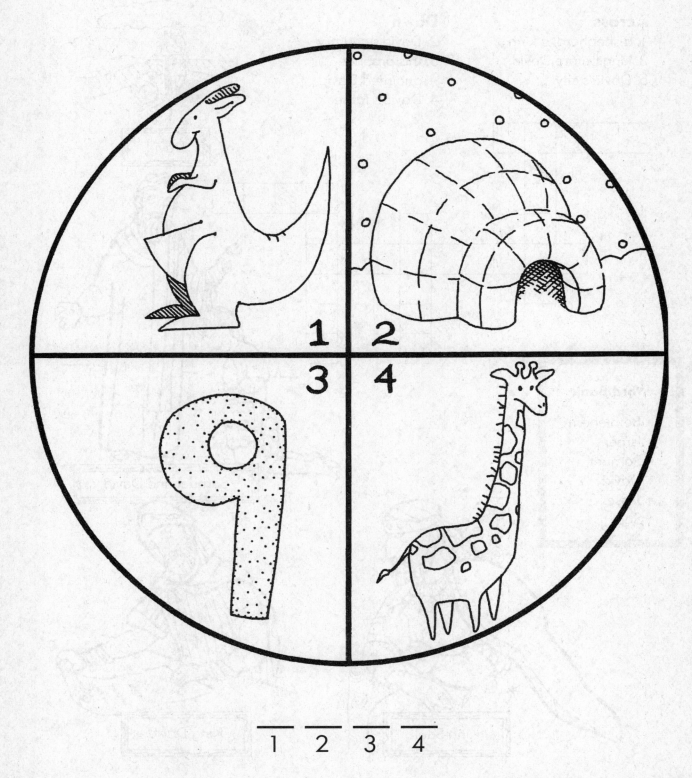

$$\overline{\rule{1cm}{0.4pt}} \quad \overline{\rule{1cm}{0.4pt}} \quad \overline{\rule{1cm}{0.4pt}} \quad \overline{\rule{1cm}{0.4pt}}$$
1   2   3   4

Crossword

Fill in the crossword with the answers to the clues. Use the Word Bank for help.

Across
1. a shepherd, a king
3. king before David
5. David's city

Down
2. David's country
3. this prophet anointed David
4. David's father

David

Samuel and David

King Saul

King David

Word Bank

- Bethlehem
- Israel
- Samuel
- David
- Jesse
- Saul

David's Choice

When David stepped out to fight Goliath, he took with him only five stones and a sling. People must have thought that David was crazy even to *think* about facing such a huge man. Imagine that you are David, trying to make the decision. Read the statements below. Beside each one, make a plus sign if it is a reason for you *to* fight Goliath; make a minus sign if it is a reason for you *not to* fight him.

Of all the reasons listed, which is the one that helped David make his important choice? What would you have done?

____ You need to get back to tending your sheep.

____ Goliath is over 9 feet tall.

____ You are just a boy.

____ You have killed a lion and a bear by yourself.

____ No one else will fight Goliath.

____ Goliath has a full suit of armor.

____ Saul's armor is too big for you.

____ All you have is a sling.

____ You could be killed.

____ There is a great reward for defeating Goliath.

____ Goliath has openly spoken against God.

____ You have God on your side.

David Riddle

What did David do when he faced Goliath on the battlefield? To answer the riddle, start with the letter *H* (at the arrow) and write down every other letter until you have moved clockwise around the square two times.

H _ _ _ _ _ _ _ _ _ _ _ _ _ _

_ _ _ _ _ _ _ _ _ .

Search the Picture

David went to fight Goliath with only a sling and five smooth stones. *Sling* and *stone* begin with the letter s. Circle everything in the picture that begins with *s*.

Warrior Word Search

Goliath was a mighty Philistine soldier. Find these five things that Goliath carried with him into battle.

- SWORD - SHIELD - ARMOR - HELMET - SPEAR

Count the Stones

David went to fight Goliath with only a sling and five smooth stones. Can you find all five stones?

Connect the Dots

King Saul became jealous of David and tried to hurt him. Where did David hide?

David and Jonathan

Color this picture of Jonathan being a good friend to David.

Straight As an Arrow

Jonathan shot an arrow as a message for David. Help Jonathan's arrow get through the maze so David will know the message.

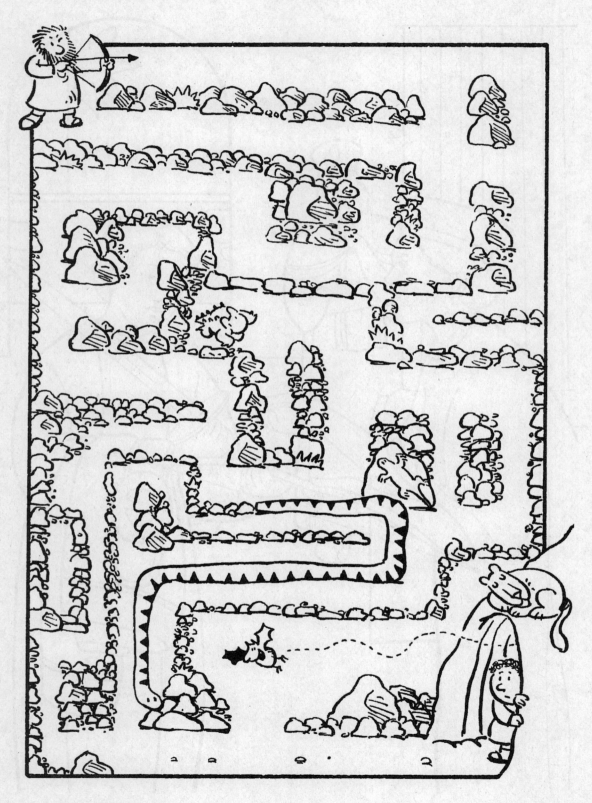

Maze

Abigail brought David and his men gifts of food. Help Abigail get through the maze to David.

START

FINISH

Color by Number

After Saul died, David became king of Israel. Use the code to color the picture.

1=PURPLE   2=YELLOW   3=BROWN   4=RED   5=BLUE

Find the Word

King Solomon asked God for only one thing. To find what Solomon wanted, color every shape that has a crown in it.

King Solomon

Solomon wanted a special place to worship God. Use the code to find out what special place Solomon built.

1=P	2=L	3=E	4=T	5=M

___ ___ ___ ___ ___ ___
 4   3   5   1   2   3

God Helping a Helper

Sometimes the people of Israel worshipped idols. Once, to punish them, God sent a famine. But God took care of His good servant Elijah. God gave him meat and bread to eat. Use a black crayon to color the spaces that have an *X* in them. You will discover what carried the food to Elijah.

1 Kings 17   149

Finish the Picture

Draw the birds bringing bread and meat to Elijah.

Word Wheel

God told the _____ to bring food to Elijah. Use the first letter of each picture to spell out the answer.

___ ___ ___ ___ ___ ___
1   2   3   4   5   6

God Shows His Power

Elijah prayed, and God sent fire to show his power. Finish this picture by drawing fire on top of the altar. Then color the picture.

Telling the Truth

King Jehoshaphat and King Ahab asked 400 prophets whether or not they should go to battle against the army of Aram. Only God's prophet Micaiah told the truth. Using the code, write what Micaiah told the kings. Then read 1 Kings 22:1-28 to know the whole story.

Picture Crossword

God took Elijah to Heaven in a chariot of fire. Write the words in the correct puzzle space.

God Heals Naaman

Elisha told Naaman to dip in the Jordan River seven times and he would be healed. Color this picture of Naaman after God healed him.

Tell Hezekiah's Story

Choose the words in the Word Bank to fit in the blanks. Then take the letters inside the shapes and complete the sentence at the bottom of the page. Read 2 Kings 20:1-11 to check your answers.

(v. 1) __ __ __ __ __ 🌲 __ became very ill.

(v. 1) The __ __ ⭐ __ __ __ __ Isaiah went to see him.

(v. 2) Hezekiah turned toward the __ __ ▽ __ and

__ ☐ __ __ __ ☁ to the Lord.

(v. 4) The Lord spoke his word to __ __ __ __ __ __ .

(v. 5) "Go back and tell Hezekiah, . . .

'I have heard your __ __ __ ◇ __ __ .'"

(v. 8) Hezekiah asked, "What will be the ♡ __ __ __

that the Lord will heal me?"

(v. 10) Hezekiah answered,

"Have [the shadow] go back ten ⧗ __ __ __ __ ."

Word Bank

- prayed
- Hezekiah
- Isaiah
- prayer
- sign
- steps
- wall
- prophet

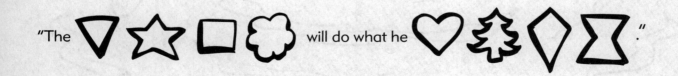

"The ▽ ☆ ☐ ☁ will do what he ♡ 🌲 ◇ ⧗ "

King Josiah Rebus

Color the pictures in the rebus. Use the rebus to retell the story of King Josiah obeying the law. See the picture descriptions for what each picture stands for.

King Josiah   God   Shaphan   Temple   Book of the Law   People

 was 8 years old when he became king. He was a good king who always did what was right in the eyes of . When was 26 years old, he sent to the . wanted workers to repair the . Hilkiah, the high priest, told that he had found the in the . read the and then read the to . When heard the words of the book, he was sad because he knew that he and his had not been doing what wanted. called the high priest, , and some other men together and asked them to ask what he wanted. called his together and read them all the words in the . and the agreed to obey .

2 Kings 22   157

Josiah Reads God's Word

What was Josiah's job? Connect the dots to find out.

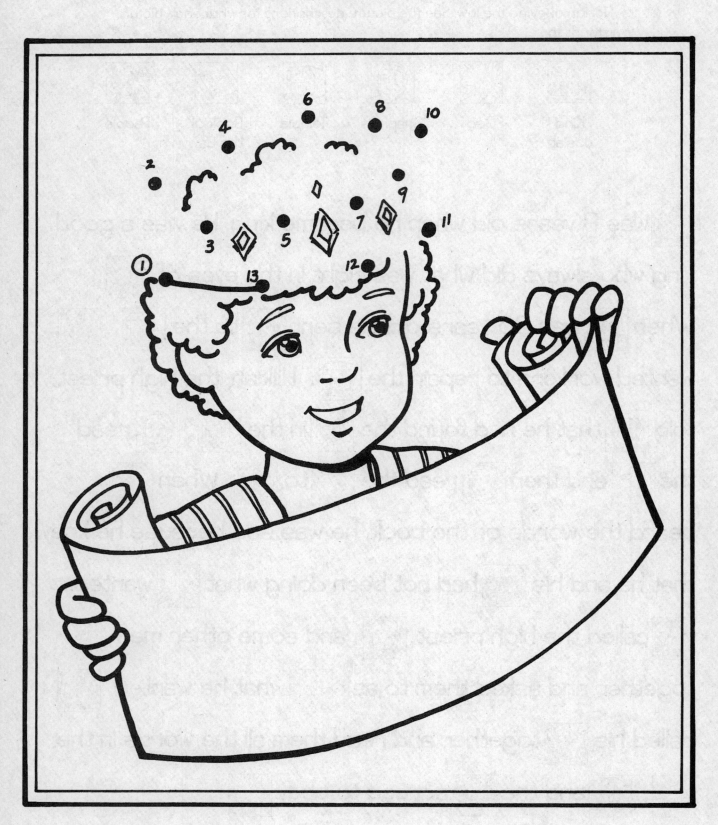

Jehoshaphat Prays

Color this picture of King Jehoshaphat leading the people in praying for God's help.

2 Chronicles 20

The Secret of Success

Uzziah became king when he was only 16 years old, yet he was a successful and powerful ruler for many years. How did he do it? Use these charts to find out. At the top of each column, write the letter indicated by the black square in the box. (See 2 Chronicles 26:1-5.)

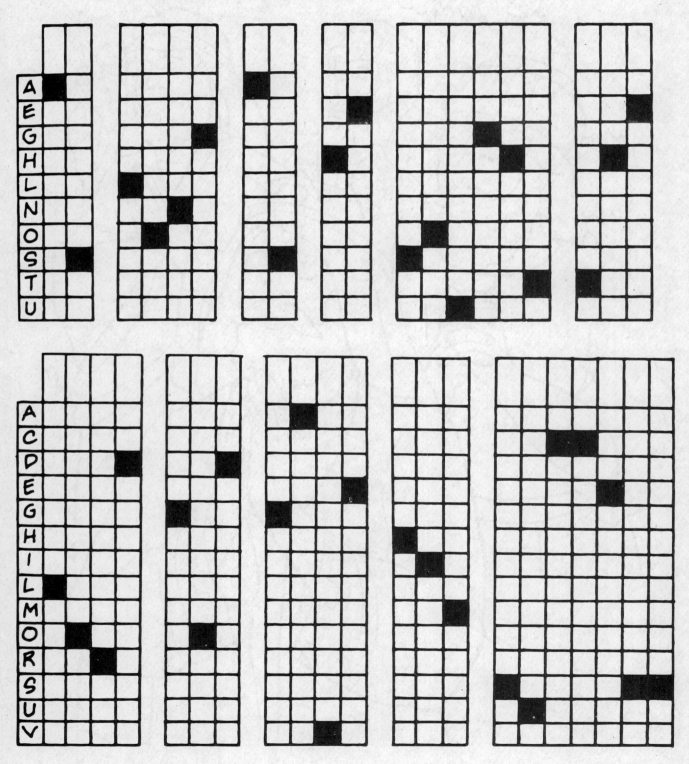

Nehemiah Maze

Color the maze. Draw a line through the maze as you retell the story of Nehemiah rebuilding the walls of Jerusalem. Make sure you pass all of the markers, in order, along the way.

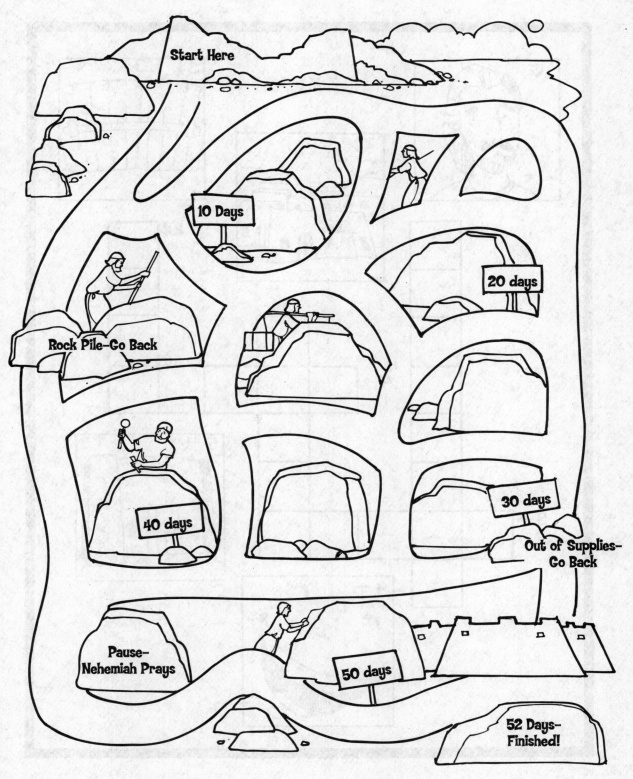

Start Here

10 Days

20 days

Rock Pile-Go Back

40 days

30 days

Out of Supplies-
Go Back

Pause-
Nehemiah Prays

50 days

52 Days-
Finished!

Picture Crossword

Nehemiah helped the people rebuild the walls of Jerusalem. Write the words in the correct puzzle space.

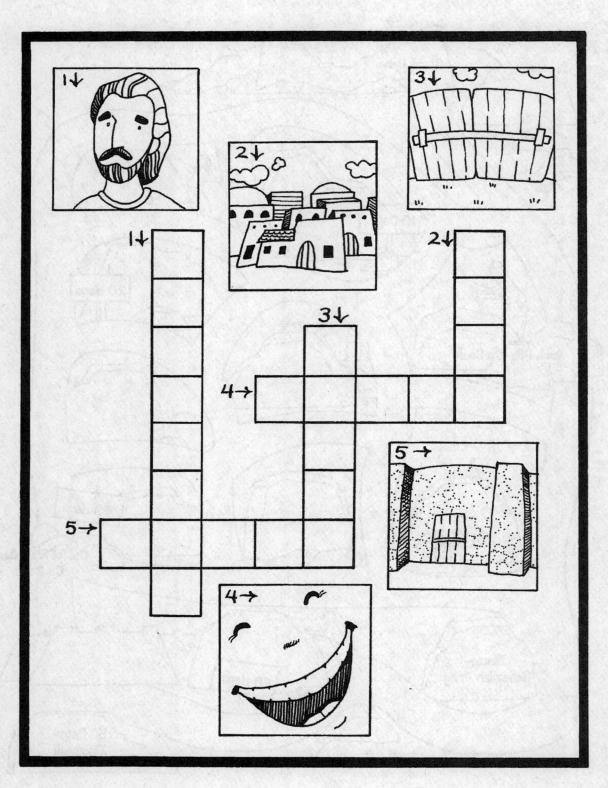

Nehemiah Rebuilds the Wall

Finish this picture by drawing higher walls around the city of Jerusalem.

Queen Esther

The real-life events of Queen Esther are exciting! Find the following words in the word search.

- Mordecai
- Esther
- Jews
- Haman
- hanged
- king
- gate
- cousin
- scepter
- banquet

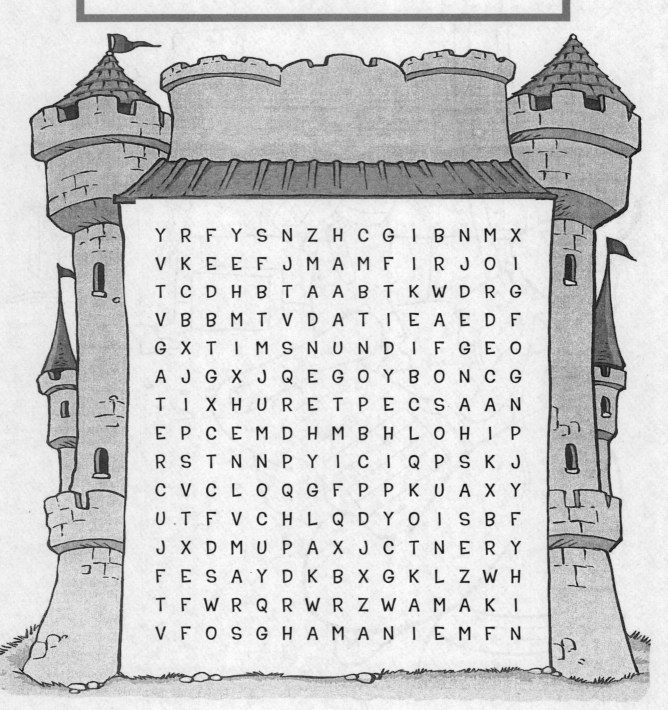

Y R F Y S N Z H C G I B N M X
V K E E F J M A M F I R J O I
T C D H B T A A B T K W D R G
V B B M T V D A T I E A E D F
G X T I M S N U N D I F G E O
A J G X J Q E G O Y B O N C G
T I X H U R E T P E C S A A N
E P C E M D H M B H L O H I P
R S T N N P Y I C I Q P S K J
C V C L O Q G F P P K U A X Y
U T F V C H L Q D Y O I S B F
J X D M U P A X J C T N E R Y
F E S A Y D K B X G K L Z W H
T F W R Q R W R Z W A M A K I
V F O S G H A M A N I E M F N

Finish the Picture

Finish the picture of Queen Esther. Use the colors below.

1=RED   2=YELLOW   3=GREEN   4=PURPLE
5=BLUE   6=BROWN   7=BLACK

Picture Match-Up

Esther became the queen of Persia. Draw a line between the two pictures of Esther that are alike.

What's Wrong Here?

Esther talked to the king to save the Jewish people. Circle five silly things in the picture.

Job Riddle

What person in the Bible was most like a doctor? To answer the riddle, use the decoder to change each number to a letter.

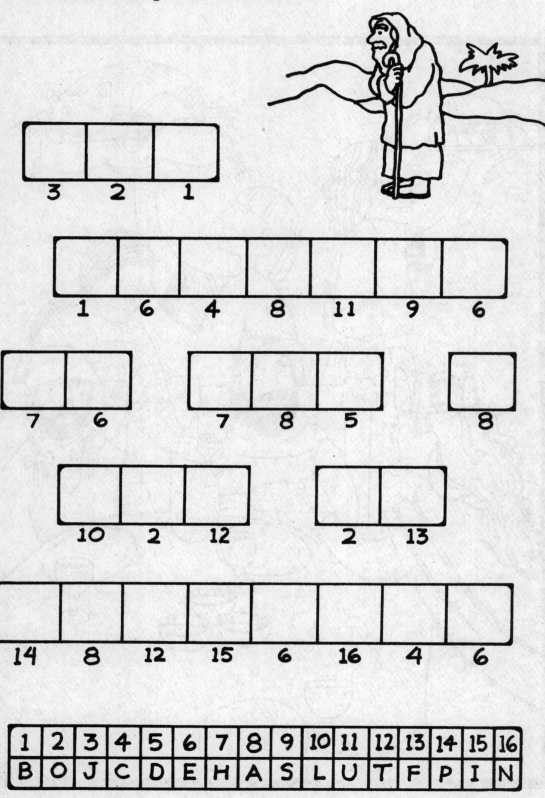

Row 1: 3 2 1

Row 2: 1 6 4 8 11 9 6

Row 3: 7 6 | 7 8 5 | 8

Row 4: 10 2 12 | 2 13

Row 5: 14 8 12 15 6 16 4 6

1	2	3	4	5	6	7	8	9	10	11	12	13	14	15	16
B	O	J	C	D	E	H	A	S	L	U	T	F	P	I	N

Musical Praise

David loved to write songs and poems to God. Use the code to find out which book of the Bible is full of David's songs.

__ __ __ __ __ __
4   5   2   3   1   5

David Match-Up

David loved to talk to God. Many of David's prayers are in the book of Psalms. Find the two pictures of David praying that are the same.

Lost Sheep

Find the misspelled letter in each sheep's name taken from Psalm 23. Put the correct letter in the blank below with the same number.

Who is our shepherd? ___ ___ ___ ___ ___ ___ ___
1   2   3   4   5   6   7

1
pash<u>u</u>res

2
nott<u>i</u>ng

3
gre<u>a</u>n

4
<u>r</u>eads

5
s<u>t</u>ul

6
wat<u>e</u>ms

7
goot<u>t</u>ness

How Many Sheep?

One of David's most-loved songs is Psalm 23. It tells us that God takes care of us like a shepherd takes care of his sheep. How many sheep do you see?

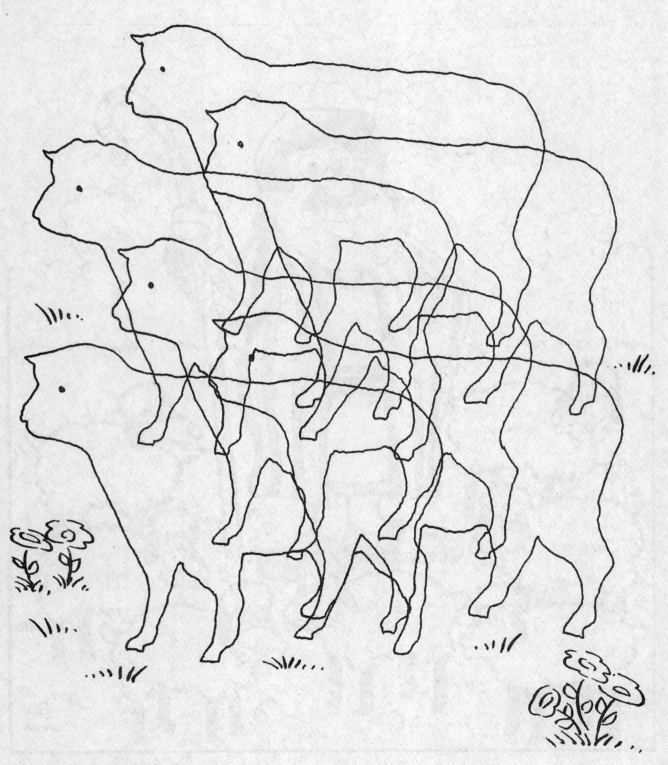

Maze

Ants are hard workers! The Bible says we should learn from them. Help these ants find their way back to the anthill.

When the Lord Calls

What did Isaiah say when he heard the voice of the Lord calling for someone to do God's work? Isaiah's answer, which should be our answer too, is hidden in this puzzle. Color all the spaces containing a dot to make the answer appear. You can find the answer in Isaiah 6:8.

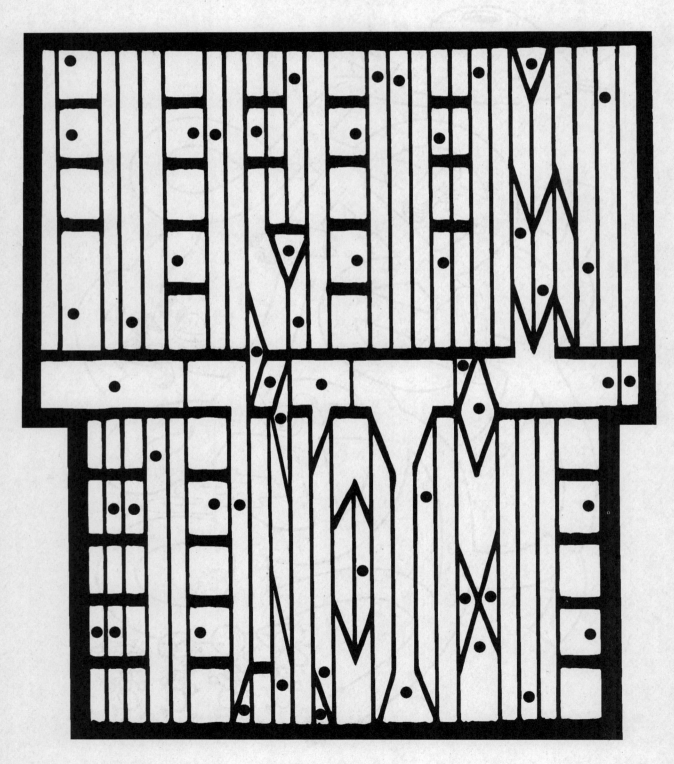

Read the Message

What did God say that Jesus would be called? Use the code to find out.

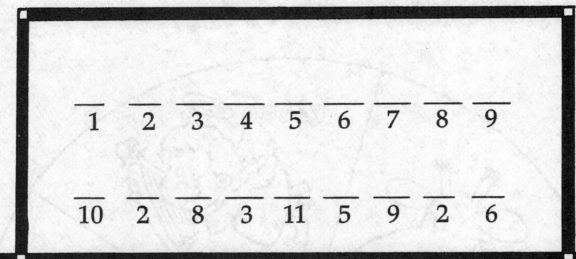

$$\overline{}_{1} \quad \overline{}_{2} \quad \overline{}_{3} \quad \overline{}_{4} \quad \overline{}_{5} \quad \overline{}_{6} \quad \overline{}_{7} \quad \overline{}_{8} \quad \overline{}_{9}$$

$$\overline{}_{10} \quad \overline{}_{2} \quad \overline{}_{8} \quad \overline{}_{3} \quad \overline{}_{11} \quad \overline{}_{5} \quad \overline{}_{9} \quad \overline{}_{2} \quad \overline{}_{6}$$

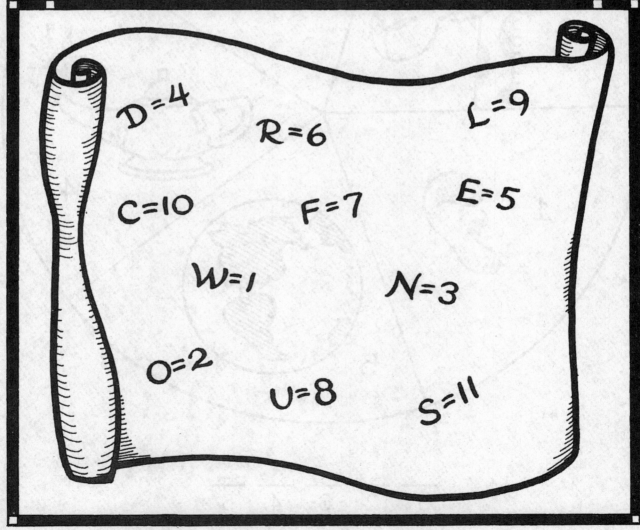

D=4
R=6
L=9
C=10
F=7
E=5
W=1
N=3
O=2
U=8
S=11

Word Wheel

The Bible says that people who trust God will be strong like the _____ in the sky. Use the word wheel to complete the sentence. Write the first letter of the pictures in the spaces below.

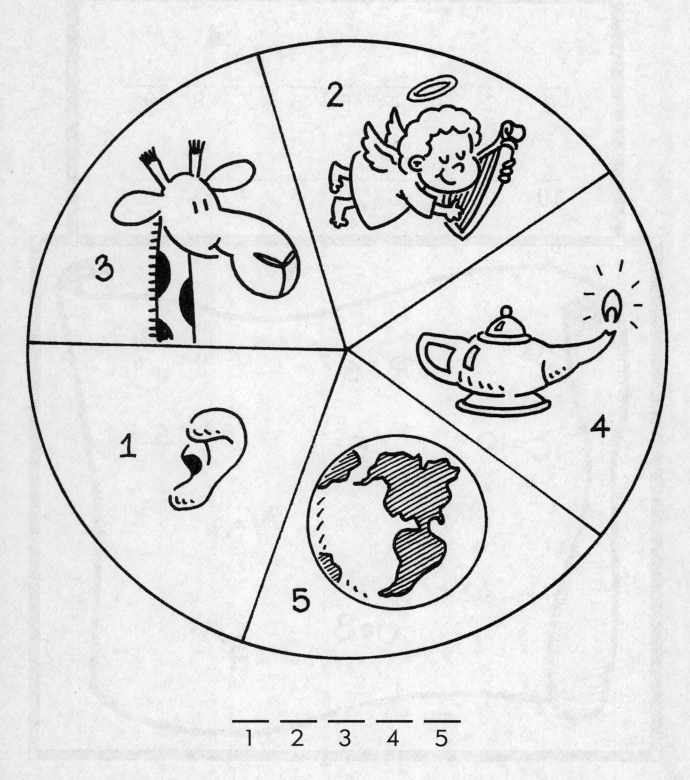

 __ __ __ __ __
 1   2   3   4   5

Finish the Picture

Daniel and his friends obeyed God by only eating the good food that God wanted them to eat. Finish this picture by drawing some of the good food they might have eaten.

Find-a-Word Furnace

Check among the flames and see if you can find these words from the Bible story about Shadrach, Meshach, and Abednego found in Daniel 3. Look up, down, and across.

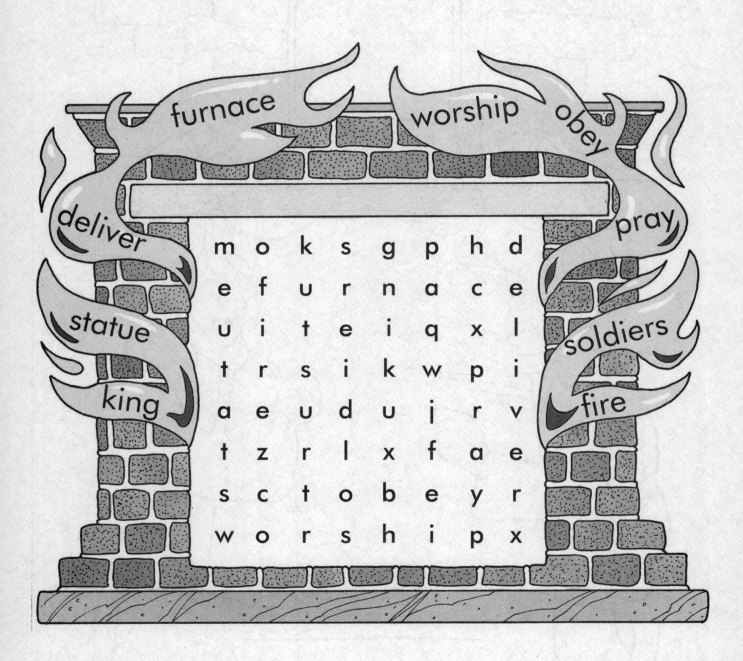

furnace
worship
obey
deliver
pray
statue
soldiers
king
fire

m o k s g p h d
e f u r n a c e
u i t e i q x l
t r s i k w p i
a e u d u j r v
t z r l x f a e
s c t o b e y r
w o r s h i p x

Three Brave Friends

To find out what Shadrach, Meshach, and Abednego told the king, color in the empty spaces. You can check your answer in Daniel 3:18.

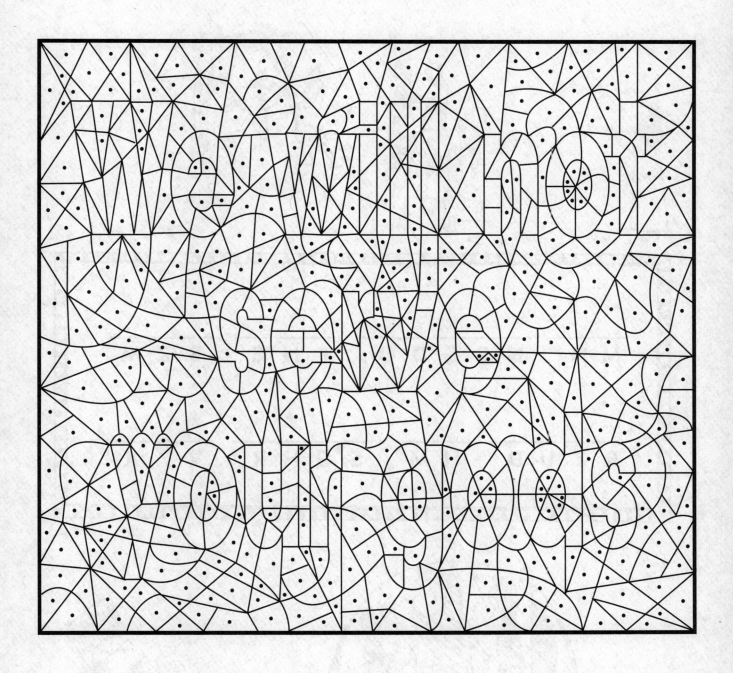

Rescued!

What did the king say when God rescued Shadrach, Meshach, and Abednego from the fiery furnace? Above each letter, write the letter that comes after it in the alphabet. Hint: After Z comes A.

MN   NSGDQ   FNC   BZM

RZUD   HM   SGHR   VZX !

Daniel and the Lions

Color this picture of Daniel in the lions' den. God protected Daniel and he was not hurt.

Finish the Picture

Daniel was thrown into a den of hungry lions. Use the boxes to finish the picture of the lion.

Daniel and the Lions' Den

The Bible doesn't tell us exactly what happened inside the lions' den the night Daniel was there. It's fun to consider what Daniel and the lions might have been thinking or doing. Fill in the word balloons next to Daniel and the lions in the cartoon below, showing what might have been on their minds.

In the Lions' Den

God sent someone to help Daniel in the lions' den. Who was it? Color all the boxes that have a lion. Place the first letter of each picture that is not a lion on the lines below.

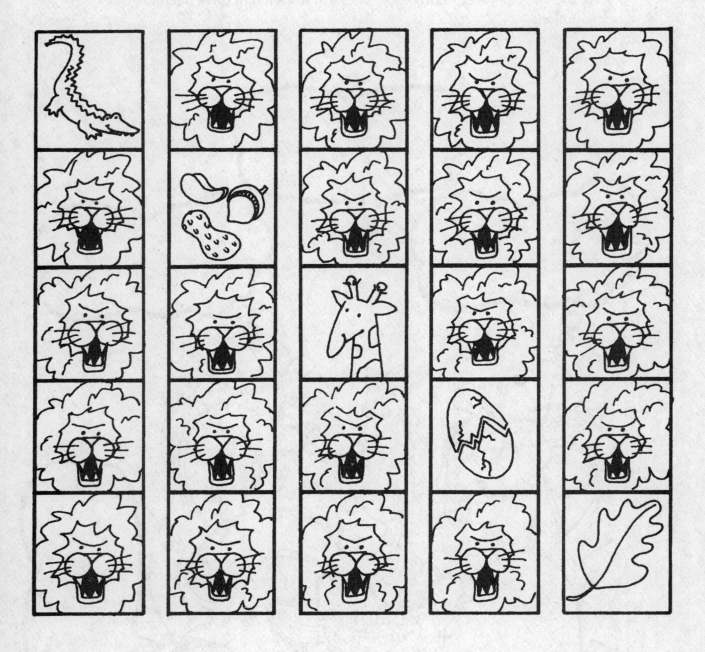

___ ___ ___ ___ ___

Picture Search

An angel protected Daniel from the hungry lions. Find these pictures in the box in the same order as below. Look up, down, and across.

Daniel Riddle

If there were ten lions in the den with Daniel, what time was it? To answer the riddle, write the last letter of each picture clue in the correct space below.

Oh, No, Jonah!

God gave Jonah a job to do, but Jonah didn't want to do it. When Jonah tried to run away to Tarshish, he got into trouble. Help Jonah find his way to Joppa and then on to Nineveh so he can do what God asked him to do. You can read Jonah's story in Jonah 1–3.

Jonah and the Big Fish

It's hard to imagine what it might have been like for Jonah inside the fish. Pretend that you are Jonah. Try to describe your experience by finishing the following sentences.

It smelled _____.

It looked _____.

The temperature was _____.

I saw lots of _____.

I couldn't _____.

I felt like _____.

I wanted _____.

Jonah Riddle

How did Jonah feel after he was swallowed by the big fish? To answer the riddle, cross out the letters in each line that appear two times.

S L I K E S

T H E T W A S

P I N P W A Y

C O V E R C H I S

R H E A D R

Go to Nineveh

Help Jonah go to Nineveh to give God's message to the people.

Jonah 3

Number Code

Long before Jesus was born, Micah the prophet wrote that Jesus would be born in _____. Use the number code to finish the sentence.

 __ __ __ __ __ __ __ __ __
 4   2   6   1   3   2   1   2   5

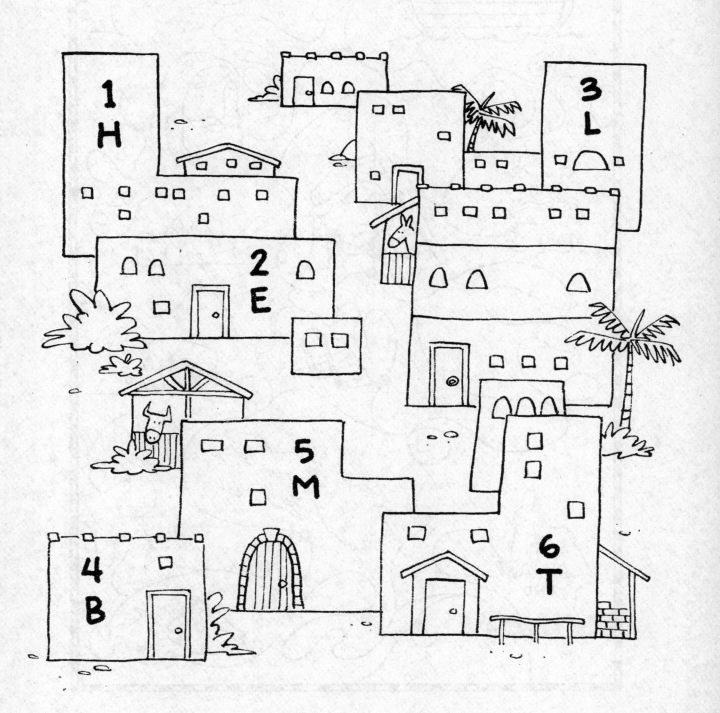

Time Travels

Find your way from creation to the next Old Testament event.

Word Search

Find the names of Jesus' parents and some of his other relatives in this word search. Look up, down, across, and backwards.

MARY

JOSEPH

DAVID

RUTH

```
Z A R U T H G O Q
P C B O D N C D H
D G T Q N G T Q P
A A B R A H A M E
V L T H S A F S S
I M D N A W G M O
D T M A R Y R S J
E V T O A G F K Y
R V H W H L J H I
```

ABRAHAM

SARAH

Picture Code

Another name for Jesus means "God with us." Write the first letter of the name of each picture on the lines below.

__ __ __ __ __ __ __ __
1 2 3 4 5 6 7 8

1

2

3

4

5

6

7

8

Mary Praises God

Color the pictures in the rebus. Use the rebus to retell the story of Mary praising God after she received the news that she would be Jesus' mother. See the picture descriptions for what each picture stands for.

Gabriel   Mary   Baby   Elizabeth

God sent the angel [Gabriel] to speak to [Mary]. [Gabriel] told [Mary] that

God was pleased with her. He told her that she would have

a [Baby] and should name him Jesus. [Gabriel] told [Mary] that the [Baby]

would be the Son of God. [Gabriel] also told [Mary] that her

cousin [Elizabeth] was going to have a [Baby] too, even though [Elizabeth] was

old. [Gabriel] said nothing is impossible with God. [Mary] said that

she was the Lord's servant. [Mary] went to visit [Elizabeth]. When they

greeted each other, the [Baby] inside [Elizabeth] jumped for joy! [Elizabeth]

knew that God had blessed [Mary]. [Mary] sang a song of

praise to God.

Word Scramble

An angel told Mary that she would have a baby. Unscramble the letters to find out who the baby was.

ODSG ONS SUEJS

__ __ __'__ __ __ __,

__ __ __ __ __

Word Search

An angel came to Mary with special news from God. Find these words in the puzzle. Look up, across, and down.

- ANGEL
- GABRIEL
- BABY
- JESUS
- MARY
- SON OF GOD

A	X	H	Y	T	W	O
D	A	N	G	E	L	B
O	Z	S	A	K	P	Q
G	I	O	B	A	B	Y
F	M	A	R	Y	S	D
O	N	Y	I	W	U	J
N	O	P	E	C	S	K
O	X	B	L	R	E	P
S	P	D	E	F	J	O

Shadow Match-Up

Mary may have ridden on a donkey to Bethlehem. Match the picture to the correct shadow.

What's Wrong Here?

Mary and Joseph went to Bethlehem. Circle five things that don't belong in the picture.

Busy Bethlehem

Help Mary and Joseph find their way through the crowd to the inn.

Color by Number

Color the picture using the numbers and the chart. Who is in the picture?

1=BLUE	3=BROWN	5=BLACK	7=GREEN
2=YELLOW	4=ORANGE	6=PURPLE	

Jesus Is Born

Tell how God cared for little Jesus. Use the words to fill in the puzzle.

People names go
across:
• Jesus
• angel
• Herod
• Joseph

Place names go
down:
• Nazareth
• Egypt
• Bethlehem

What's Wrong?

Jesus was born in a stable in Bethlehem. How many things can you find wrong with this picture?

Connect the Dots

Mary wrapped Jesus in cloths to keep him warm. Connect the dots to make Jesus' bed, then color the picture.

Count the Sheep

Shepherds were watching their sheep on the night Jesus was born. How many sheep do you see?

Connect the Dots

What are these shepherds watching over? Connect the dots to see.

Manger Maze

Help the shepherds find baby Jesus.

A Savior

Find the angel's message to the shepherds by going through the maze.
Write the letters on the lines below, using only the letters on the correct path
to Jesus. You can check your answer by reading Luke 2:1-20.

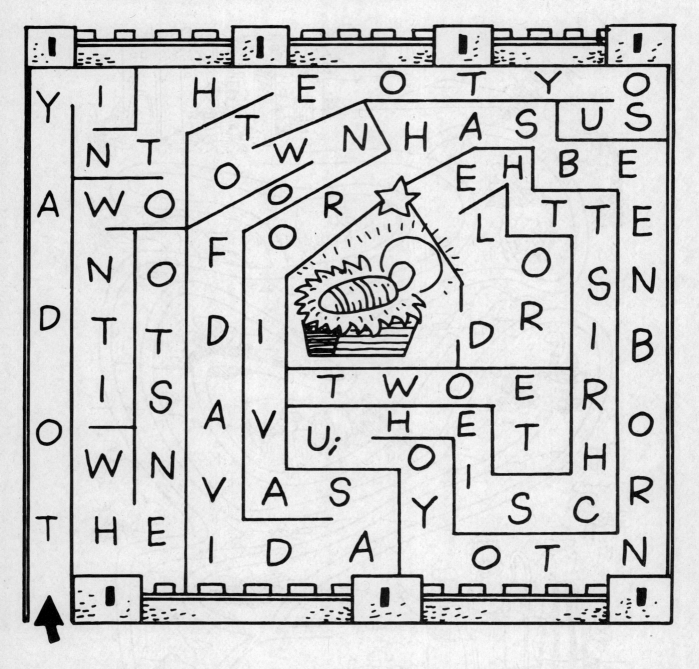

_____

_____

_____

Draw the Angel

An angel told shepherds about baby Jesus. Copy the design in each numbered square into the matching square below.

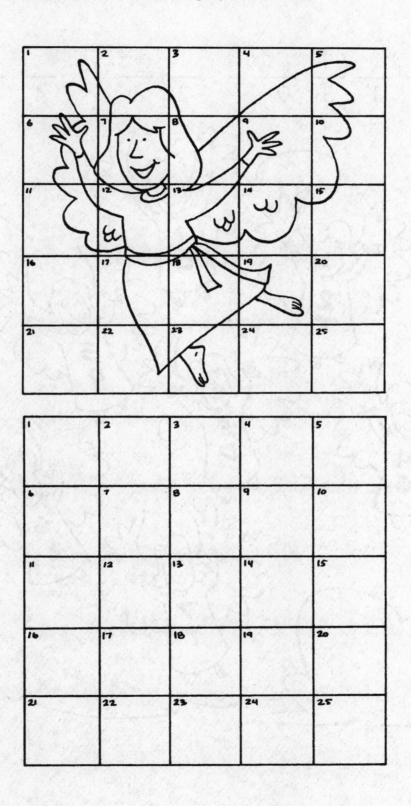

Angel Code

The angels sang and praised God. What did they say? Use the code to find out.

$$\overline{}\ \overline{}\ \overline{}\ \overline{}\ \overline{}\quad\overline{}\ \overline{}\quad\overline{}\ \overline{}\ \overline{}$$
4   6   1   3   7   2   1   4   1   5

Simeon and Anna

Color this picture of Simeon and Anna thanking God for baby Jesus.

Maze

Anna knew that baby Jesus was the Son of God. Help Anna get through the maze to see baby Jesus.

How Many Stars?

Wise men from the east followed a star to worship Jesus. How many stars do you see?

Camel Match-Up

The wise men may have ridden camels on their long trip. Circle the two camels that are the same.

Matthew 2

Follow the Star

The wise men followed a special star to find Jesus. Follow the big stars and help them find the way.

The Wise Men's Trip

Help the wise men find Jesus. Follow the directions below.

1. Go west 4 spaces.
2. Go north 6 spaces.
3. Go west 4 spaces.

4. Go north 4 spaces.
5. Go east 5 spaces.
6. Go north 3 spaces.

7. Go east 8 spaces.
8. Go north 8 spaces.
9. Go west 14 spaces.

10. Go south 8 spaces.
11. Go west 3 spaces.

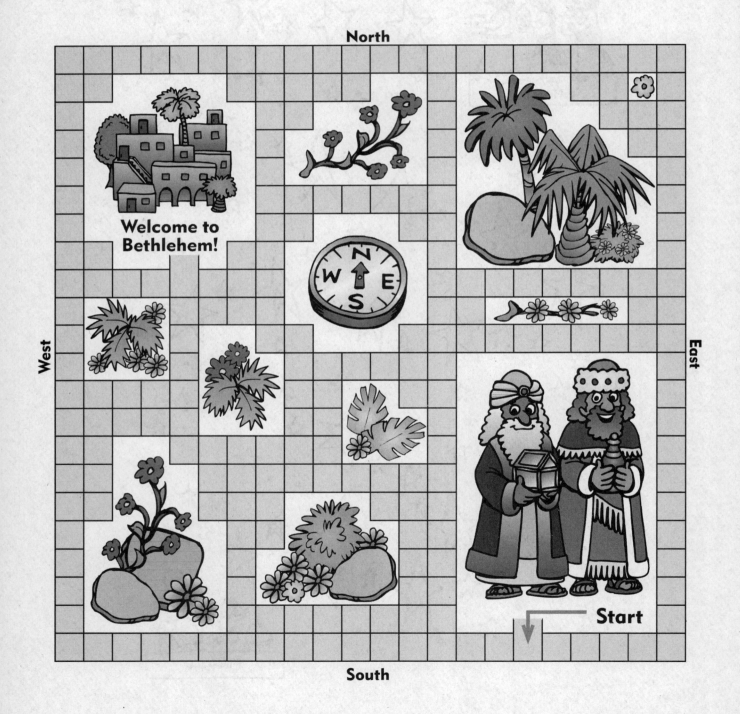

Connect the Dots

Connect the dots to see what the wise men were following.

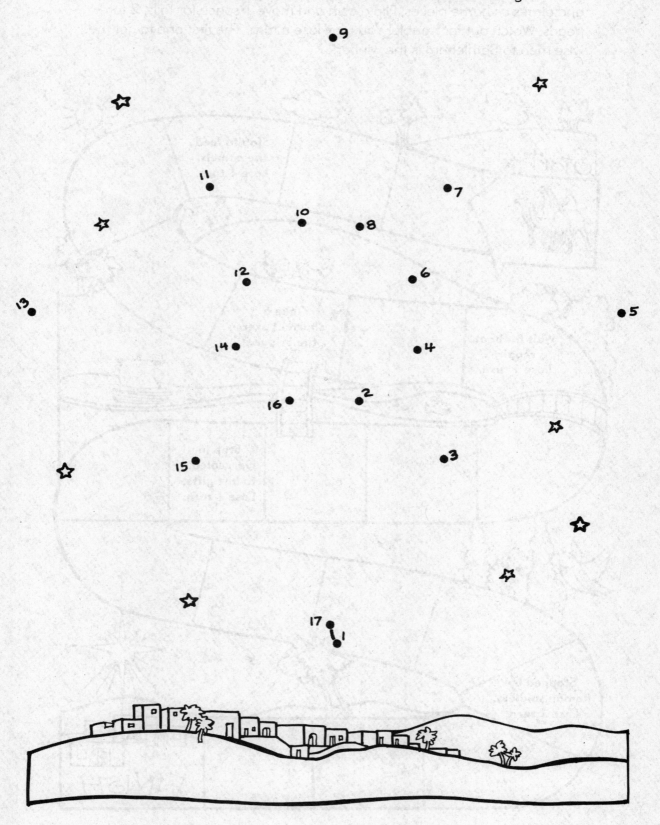

Wise Men Game

Play this game with a friend. Lay the game on a flat surface. Use pennies and dimes as game pieces. Flip a coin and move 1 space for tails, 2 for heads. Watch out for trouble! You may lose a turn. The first one to get the wise men to Bethlehem is the winner!

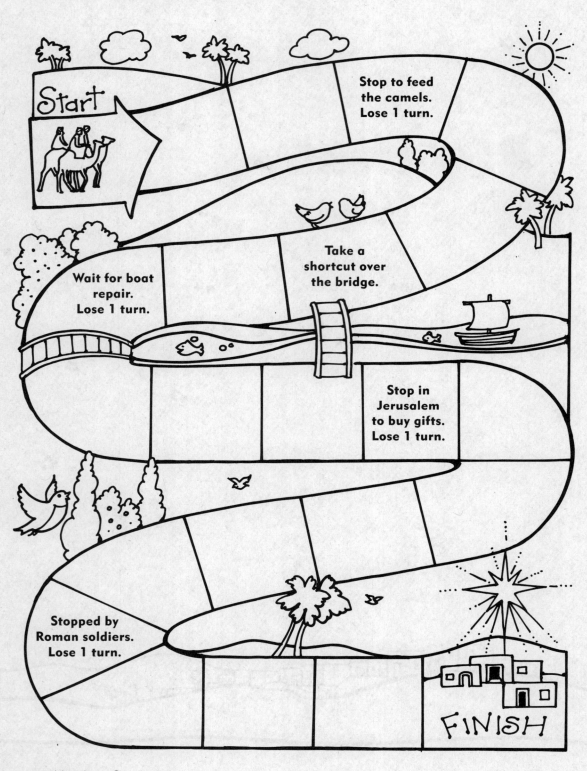

Color by Number

Color the shapes to reveal a hidden picture.

Gift Match-Up

The wise men gave gifts to Jesus. Find three pairs of gifts that are alike.

Find and Color

The wise men brought gifts to Jesus. Find and color the containers of gold, frankincense, and myrrh.

Temple Crossword

When Jesus was 12 years old, he went with Mary and Joseph to the temple. Jesus talked with the teachers about God. Write the words in the correct puzzle spaces.

Which One?

When Jesus was 12 years old, he went with Mary and Joseph to the temple in Jerusalem. Which road is the right one to take?

What's Different?

Jesus, Mary, and Joseph went to Jerusalem for Passover. Find five differences between the two pictures.

Color by Code

After Passover, Jesus stayed in Jerusalem and talked with the religious teachers. Use the color code to color the picture.

1=BLUE	4=GREEN	7=YELLOW
2=WHITE	5=PURPLE	8=GRAY
3=BROWN	6=RED	

Picture Code

Jesus said he had to be in

$$\overline{}_{1}\ \overline{}_{2}\ \overline{}_{3}\qquad \overline{}_{4}\ \overline{}_{5}\ \overline{}_{6}\ \overline{}_{7}\ \overline{}_{8}\ \overline{}_{9}'\ \overline{}_{10}$$

$$\overline{}_{11}\ \overline{}_{12}\ \overline{}_{13}\ \overline{}_{14}\ \overline{}_{15}.$$

Write the first letter of each picture to fill in the blanks.

What Was Jesus Like?

Jesus grew taller and wiser, he obeyed Mary and Joseph, and he pleased God. Find the words that describe Jesus. Look up, across, and down.

```
T   A   L   L   E   R   C
O   P   W   O   E   I   D
B   N   D   W   V   D   I
E   M   I   I   H   E   E
Y   Z   X   S   B   S   P
E   G   R   E   W   A   H
D   Q   W   R   D   E   F
B   Y   N   U   G   L   D
M   X   R   C   D   P   F
```

Finish the Picture

Finish the picture of Jesus when he was 12 years old.

John the Baptist

John the Baptist preached. He helped people get ready to listen to Jesus.
Finish the puzzle below. Write the letter that comes next in ABC order.

R	S	N	O
S	T	O	P

C	N	H	M	F
D	O	I	N	G

V	Q	N	M	F
W	R	O	N	G

R	S	■	Q	S
S	T	A	R	T

C	N	H	M	F
D	O	I	N	G

Q	H	F	G	S
R	I	G	H	T

Write the words on the lines. This is what John wanted the people to do.

___ ___ ___ ___

___ ___ ___ . ___ ___

___ ___ ___ ___ ___ .

What's Wrong?

John the Baptist told people to get ready for Jesus. Find five things wrong with this picture.

John's Poem

Use these words to fill in the blanks and complete the poem about John the Baptist. You will use each word only once.

- voice
- forgave
- sin
- desert
- locusts
- Pharisees
- honey
- Son

There once was a man called "The Baptist."
The preaching of Christ was his practice.
In the _____ he preached,
Many people he reached,
But he wasn't the sort you'd relax with.

For John was a rough, grizzly man.
His skin had a dark desert tan.
He hadn't much money,
Ate _____ and _____,
And slept cuddled up in the sand.

But John had a wonderful mission
If only the people would listen.
He served as God's _____
Announcing his choice
Of the Savior for whom they'd been wishin'.

Not everyone listened to John.
The _____ thought he was wrong
To speak about Jesus
And how he would free us
From _____ that had held us so long.

But people who chose to believe
A wonderful gift would receive.
When John baptized them,
God _____ all their sin
And gave peace they could never conceive.

John listened to God every day
And said just what God said to say.
When John's work was done,
We could all know God's _____.
Thank you, John, for preparing the way.

Picture Match-Up

John the Baptist told people that Jesus was coming soon. Draw a line to connect the two pictures of John that are the same.

Word Wheel

When John baptized Jesus, the Spirit of God came down from Heaven like a _____. Use the first letter of each picture to spell out the answer.

D   O   V   E
—   —   —   —
1   2   3   4

Read the Pictures

What did God say when Jesus was baptized? Read the words and pictures of this rebus.

Matthew 3

Jesus Match-Up

Jesus went to the Jordan River to be baptized by John. Circle the pictures of Jesus and John that are the same.

Satan Tempts Jesus

Satan took Jesus to the top of a mountain. Satan told Jesus that he could have everything if he would worship Satan. But Jesus said that he would only worship God. Finish this picture by drawing the tall mountain Jesus stood on. Then color the picture.

No! No! No!

Jesus was led by God's Spirit into the desert to spend time praying. He ate nothing for forty days and nights. When he was very hungry, Satan tried to tempt him with food. Jesus said, "No!" Then Satan tried to make him prove that he was God's Son. Jesus said, "No!" Then Satan promised to give Jesus power if he would bow down to him. Jesus said, "No!" Find the other words that Jesus used to send Satan away by coloring all the spaces containing the word "No."

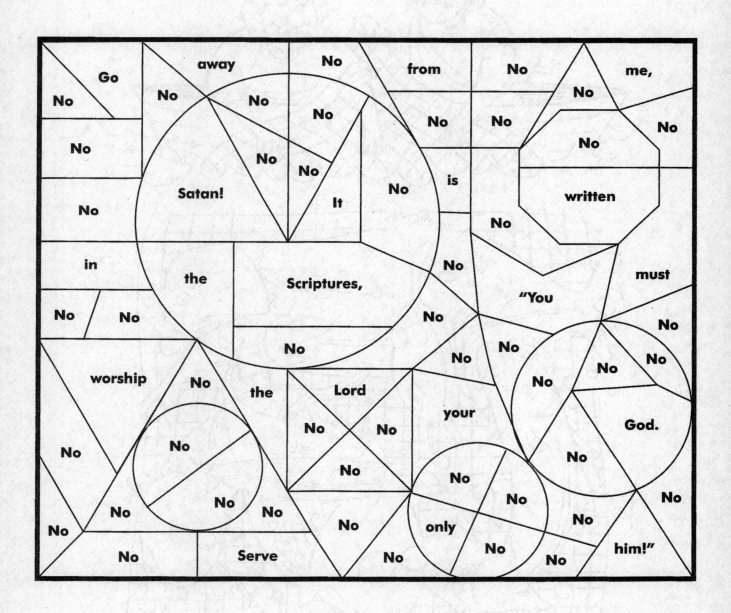

Count the Fish

Before they became Jesus' special friends, Peter and Andrew were fishermen. Count the fish that are caught in their net.

Jesus Teaches About God

Use the code to find out what man came to Jesus at night to ask him questions. Then color the picture.

__ __ __ __ __ __ __ __ __ __
4 8 7 1 6 9 5 2 3

1=O	4=N	7=C
2=U	5=M	8=I
3=S	6=D	9=E

Nicodemus Match-Up

Nicodemus came to Jesus at night to ask him some questions. Find the two pictures that are alike.

Jesus Teaches Nicodemus

Work the maze to find out what Jesus told Nicodemus.

Jesus Was Kind

Color this picture of Jesus being kind to a woman from Samaria.

It Was Amazing!

Jesus healed many people who came to him—and some who stayed home! Complete the printed letters by drawing a straight line between each dot or star and its matching dot or star. Then match each sentence to the person it describes. Read John 4:43-54 if you need help.

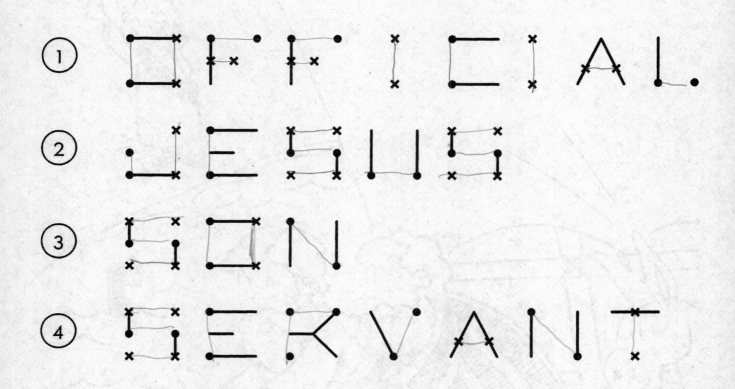

① OFFICIAL.

② JESUS

③ SON

④ SERVANT

I asked Jesus to heal my son.   ③

I told my master that his son was well.   ④

I was dying and Jesus healed me.   ②

I healed an official's sick child.   ①

What's Wrong?

Walking by Lake Galilee, Jesus invited Peter and Andrew to follow him. Circle five things wrong with this picture.

Word Search

Jesus had special friends called disciples. Find the names of four of them in the puzzle below. Look up, across, and down.

• JAMES   • JOHN   • PETER   • ANDREW

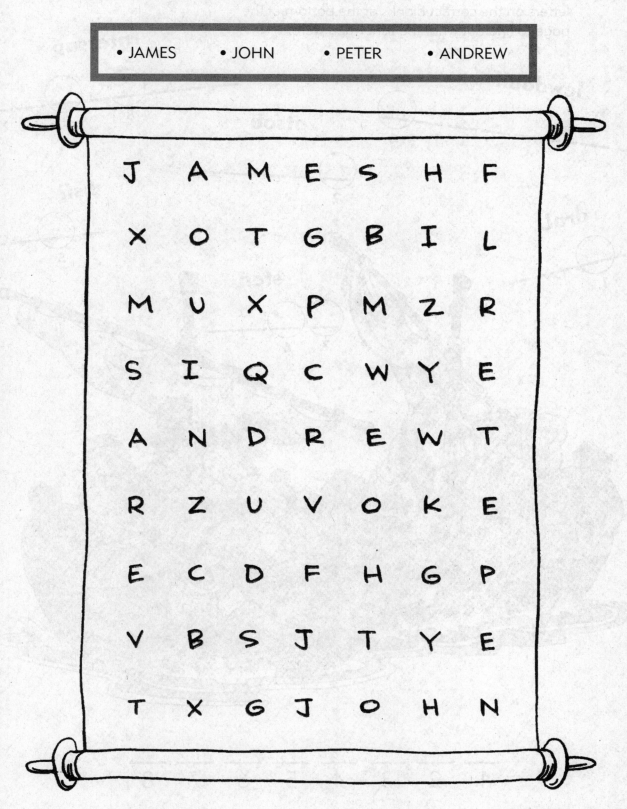

```
J  A  M  E  S  H  F
X  O  T  G  B  I  L
M  U  X  P  M  Z  R
S  I  Q  C  W  Y  E
A  N  D  R  E  W  T
R  Z  U  V  O  K  E
E  C  D  F  H  G  P
V  B  S  J  T  Y  E
T  X  G  J  O  H  N
```

Unscramble

Jesus told the fishermen to cast their nets into the water. Unscramble the words and write each word on the blanks below it. Then write the circled letters on the correct blanks at the bottom of the page to find out what the fishermen were.

rntersap

⎯ ⎯ ⎯ ⎯ ◯ ⎯ ◯ ⎯
            8   3

lewdoolf

⎯ ⎯ ⎯ ⎯ ◯ ⎯
       4

atsob

◯ ⎯ ⎯ ⎯ ⎯
2

hsfi

⎯ ⎯ ◯ ⎯
   5

droL

⎯ ◯ ⎯ ⎯
1

sten

◯ ◯ ⎯ ⎯
7 6

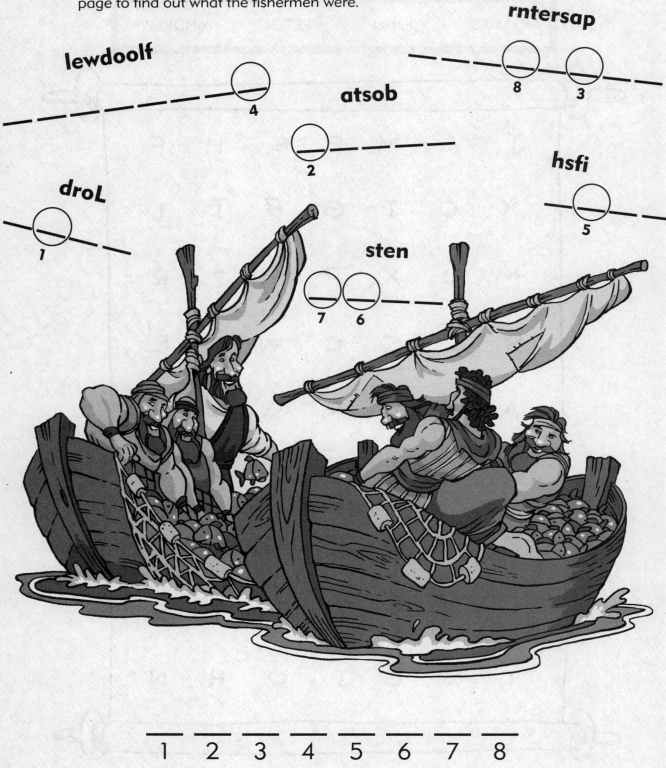

⎯ ⎯ ⎯ ⎯ ⎯ ⎯ ⎯ ⎯
1 2 3 4 5 6 7 8

Match the Catch

Jesus told the fishermen to put their nets into the water. Look at their catch! Use the code to color all the fish.

GREEN

BLUE

ORANGE

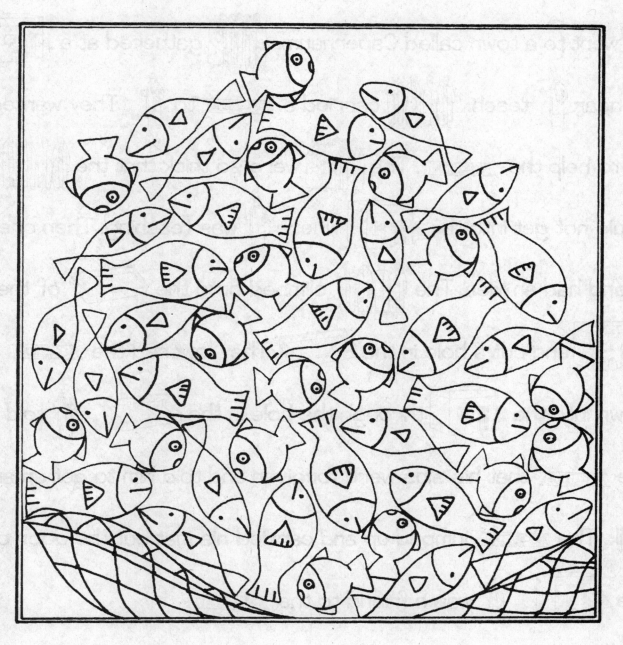

Four Friends' Rebus

Color the pictures in the rebus. Use the rebus to retell the story of Jesus healing a man who couldn't walk. See the picture descriptions for what each picture stands for.

Jesus   Crowds   Four Friends   Man Who Couldn't Walk   House   Roof

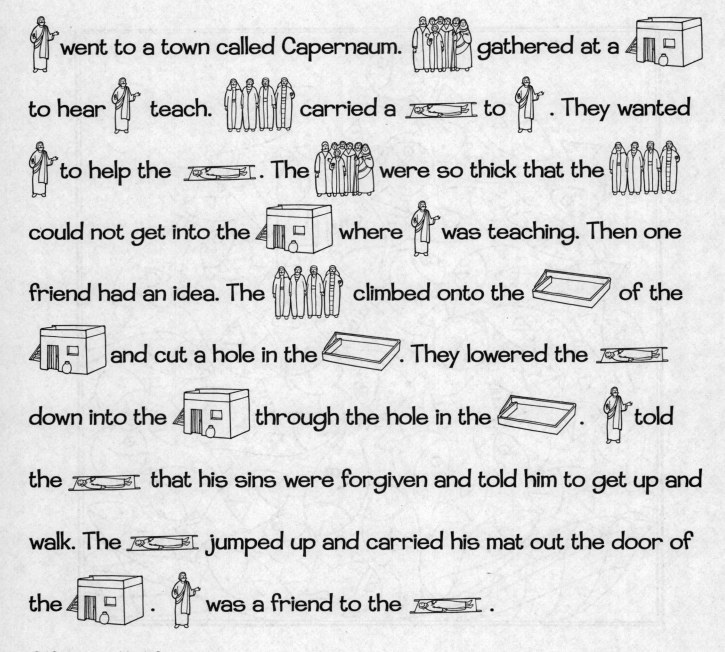

went to a town called Capernaum. gathered at a

to hear teach. carried a to . They wanted

to help the . The were so thick that the

could not get into the where was teaching. Then one

friend had an idea. The climbed onto the of the

and cut a hole in the . They lowered the

down into the through the hole in the . told

the that his sins were forgiven and told him to get up and

walk. The jumped up and carried his mat out the door of

the . was a friend to the .

Jesus Was a Friend

Place a pencil inside the dotted lines to finish the sentences.

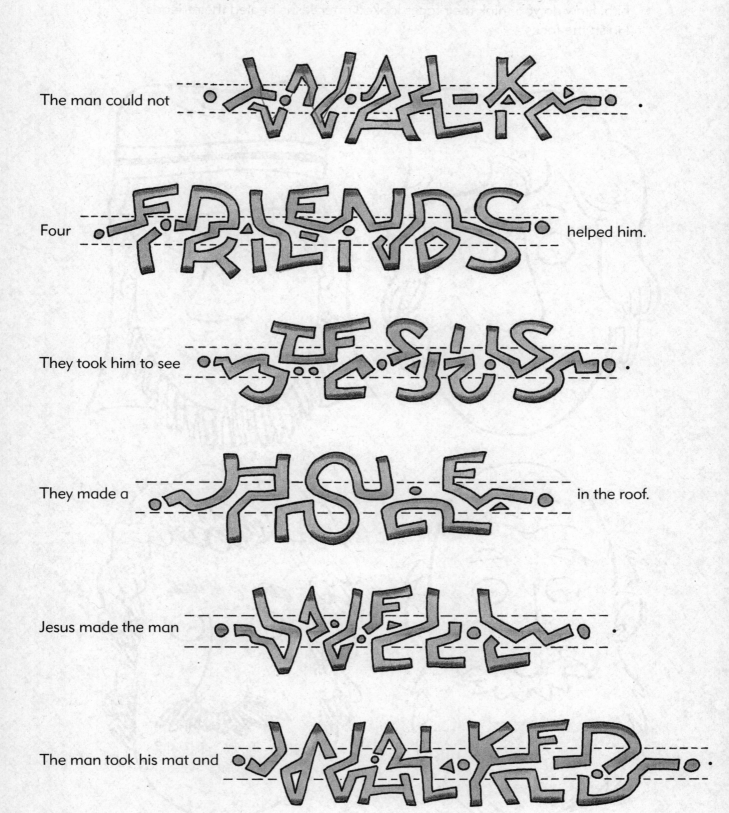

The man could not _WALK_ .

Four _FRIENDS_ helped him.

They took him to see _JESUS_ .

They made a _HOLE_ in the roof.

Jesus made the man _WELL_ .

The man took his mat and _WALKED_ .

Finish the Faces

Four men brought a friend who couldn't walk to Jesus, and Jesus healed him. How do you think their faces looked after Jesus healed their friend? Finish the faces.

Finish the Story

Use the food code to finish the story about a tax collector who chose to follow Jesus.

Jesus met a tax collector named _____ _____ _____ _____ _____ _____ _____ . Jesus told

Matthew to _____ _____ _____ _____ _____ _____ him. Matthew got up, left

_____ _____ _____ _____ _____ _____ _____ _____ _____ _____ and followed Jesus.

Matthew gave a _____ _____ _____ _____ _____ for Jesus. There were many other tax

collectors there. They were Matthew's _____ _____ _____ _____ _____ _____ _____ .

The teachers of the law began to _____ _____ _____ _____ _____ _____ _____ _____

because they said Jesus was eating with sinners. Jesus told them he came to call sinners to change

their _____ _____ _____ _____ _____ .

A- 🍎 F- 🍟 L- 🍋 P- 🍕 V- 🥕

C- 🥕 G- 🍇 M- 🍄 R- 🥕 W- 🥝

D- 🍩 H- 🍔 N- 🥒 S- 🍓 Y- 🌶

E- 🍳 I- 🧁 O- 🍊 T- 🍅

Jesus Heals

Color this picture of Jesus healing a man at a pool.

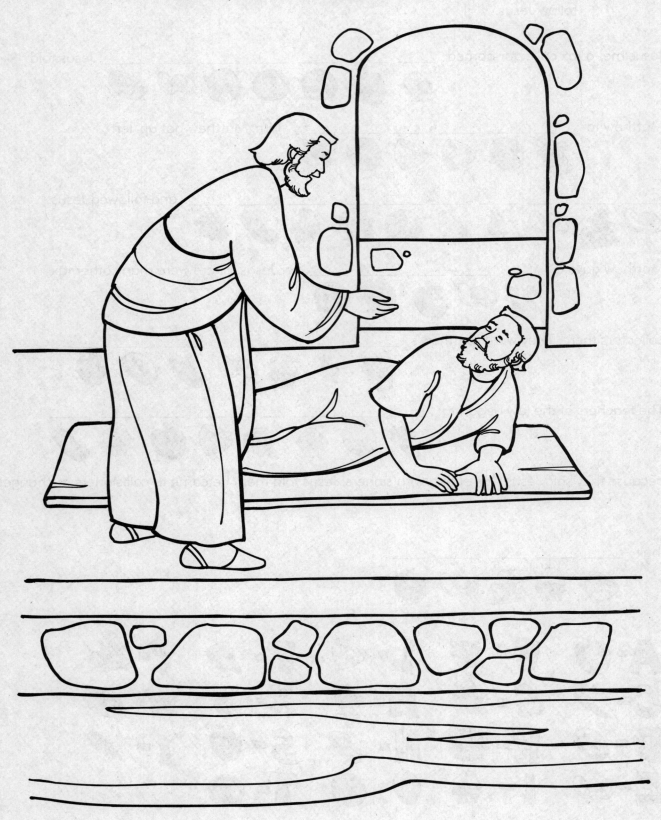

Number Code

Use the number code to find out what Jesus' friends were called.

D E S C I P L E S
3 5 2 1 5 7 6 4 2

1 = C   2 = S   3 = D   4 = E

5 = I   6 = L   7 = P

Disciple Crossword

Finish the puzzle about Jesus' disciples. Use the words in the Word Bank.

Word Bank

- Peter
- Andrew
- James
- John
- Philip
- Bartholomew
- Matthew
- Thomas
- Thaddaeus
- Simon
- James
- Judas

Follow the Path

Crowds of people came to Jesus to hear him teach. Help the people get to Jesus.

START

FINISH

Word Search

People loved to hear Jesus teach about God and his ways. Find these words in the puzzle that describe God's ways. Look up, across, and down.

- SEEK
- MERCY
- LOVE
- FORGIVE
- PEACE
- PRAY

L	W	E	U	P	T	Y
A	M	S	E	E	K	C
V	L	N	Z	K	A	R
F	O	R	G	I	V	E
P	V	I	B	D	X	M
S	E	Y	P	O	H	G
C	K	A	J	W	Q	L
O	I	R	X	B	H	U
S	K	P	E	A	C	E
O	T	I	B	D	S	W

What's Wrong?

Jesus taught a crowd of people on a hillside. Find five things wrong with this picture.

How to Pray

Decode the sentences on the left side of the page to find out some things Jesus taught about prayer. Then match each sentence to a verse in Matthew 6.

Code:
a — strawberry
d — watermelon
e — pizza
f — ice cream cone
G — cookie
h — apple
m — cherry
n — hamburger
o — banana
r — cheese
s — popsicle
v — muffin
w — pear

1. Don't S h o w o f f.

2. Don't say the s a m e things o v e r and O V E R.

3. Ask G O D for what you n e e d.

Matthew 6:11— Give us the food we need for each day.

Matthew 6:5— When you pray, don't be like the hypocrites. . . . They want people to see them pray.

Matthew 6:7— And when you pray, don't be like those people. . . . They continue saying things that mean nothing.

Picture Crossword

The wise man built his house on a rock. The foolish man built his house on sand. Write the words in the correct puzzle spaces.

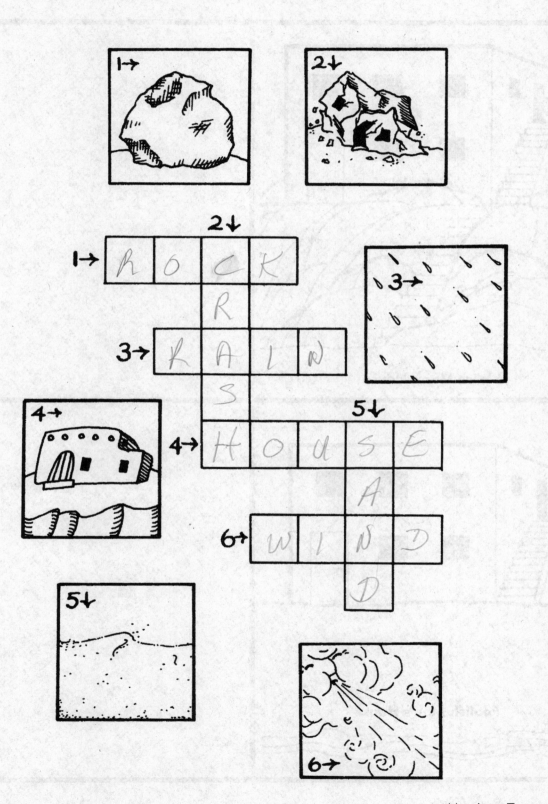

Wise and Foolish

Draw what happened to the wise man's house. Then draw what happened to the foolish man's house. You can read about this in Matthew 7:24-27.

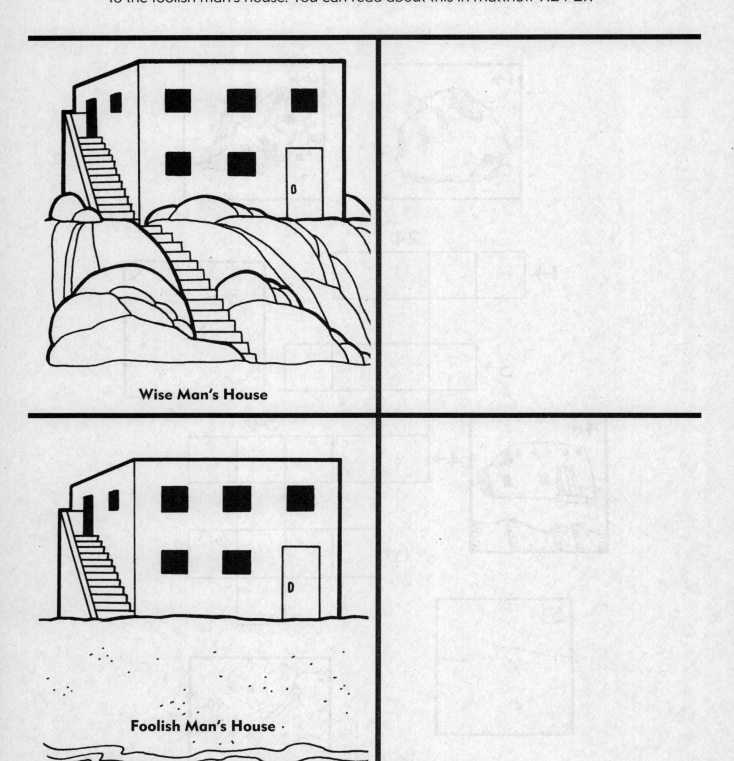

Wise Man's House

Foolish Man's House

Jesus Is a Friend

Jesus gave the woman something she really needed. Use the code to find out what Jesus gave the woman.

F O R G I V E N E S S
3 6 4 5 8 7 1 9 1 2 2

1=E   4=R   7=V
2=S   5=G   8=I
3=F   6=O   9=N

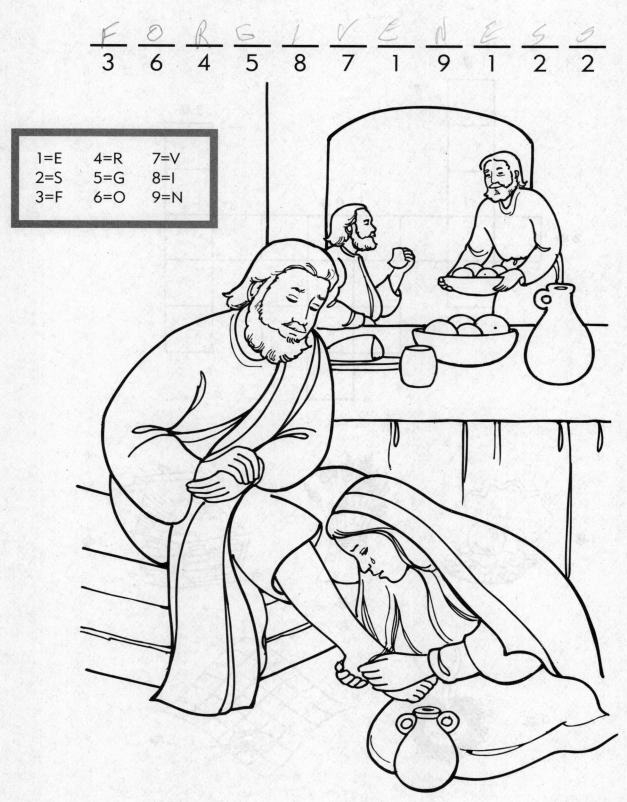

Parable Crossword

Jesus told stories called parables to describe the kingdom of God. Write the names of these pictures from the parables into the correct spaces.

Find the Way

Jesus' disciples were afraid of a storm. Help them get to the other end of the boat to wake up Jesus.

Jesus Calms a Stormy Sea

What did the disciples say about Jesus after he calmed a storm? To find out, follow the line from each letter to the empty circle and write the same letter in the circle. Read Luke 8:22-25 for help.

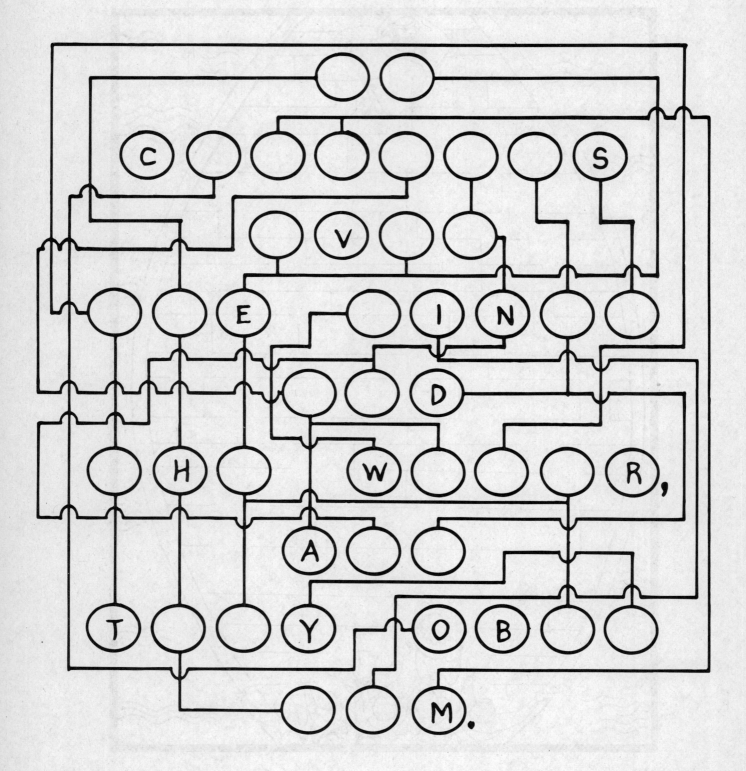

Jesus and Jairus

Help Jesus and Jairus take the correct path to get to Jairus's house.

Jairus's House

Only One Lunch

What did Andrew ask Jesus about using five loaves and two fish to feed more than 5,000 people? How was Andrew's question answered? Use the code to find out. Read John 6:1-13 to find out more.

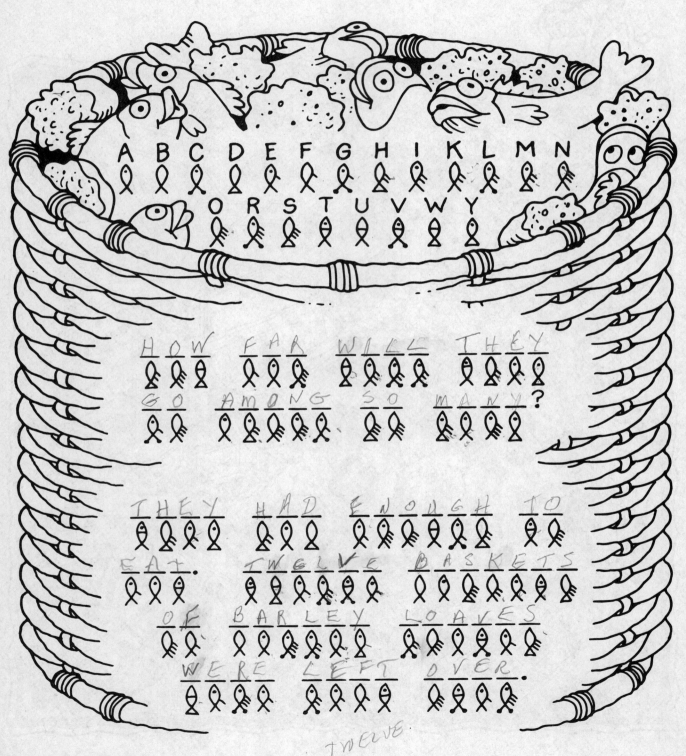

HOW FAR WILL THEY GO AMONG SO MANY?

THEY HAD ENOUGH TO EAT. TWELVE BASKETS OF BARLEY LOAVES WERE LEFT OVER.

TWELVE

Fish Match-Up

Near Bethesda, Jesus fed many people with just one boy's small lunch.
Find the two fish that are the same. Circle the bread that is different.

Fish and Bread

Jesus fed over 5,000 people with five loaves of bread and two fish. Find and circle the hidden loaves and fish in this picture. There are five loaves and five fish in the picture.

Find the Baskets

After Jesus fed the crowd near Bethesda, there were twelve baskets of leftovers. Find the baskets in the picture.

Find and Color

Jesus fed more than 5,000 people with one small lunch! Find and color all twelve baskets of leftovers.

Finish the Picture

One night, the disciples were in a boat when a big storm started. Jesus went to the disciples by walking on the water. Finish this picture by drawing Jesus walking on the water. You can read about this in Matthew 14:22-33.

Word Search

Near Tyre and Sidon, Jesus healed a woman's sick daughter. Find these words in the puzzle. Look up, across, and down.

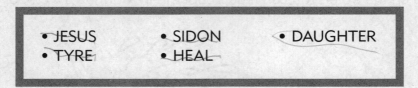

- JESUS
- TYRE
- SIDON
- HEAL
- DAUGHTER

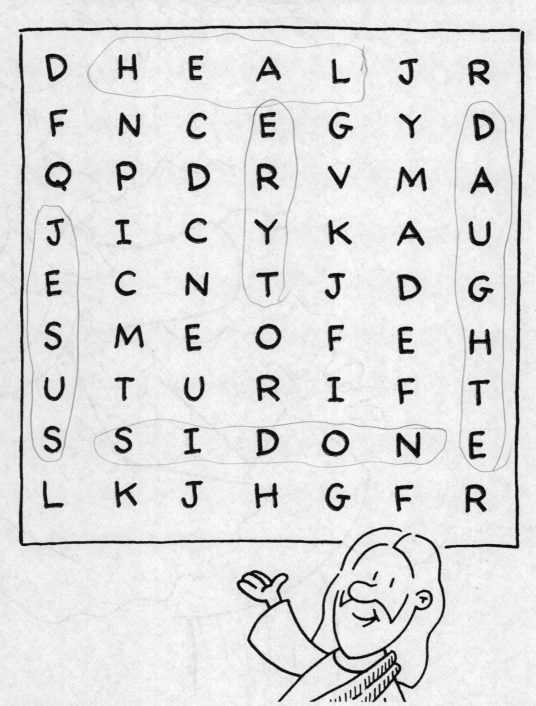

D	H	E	A	L	J	R
F	N	C	E	G	Y	D
Q	P	D	R	V	M	A
J	I	C	Y	K	A	U
E	C	N	T	J	D	G
S	M	E	O	F	E	H
U	T	U	R	I	F	T
S	S	I	D	O	N	E
L	K	J	H	G	F	R

I Can Hear!

In Mark 7:31-37, you can read about a special miracle that Jesus did. Some people brought to Jesus a man who could not hear and could not talk. His friends begged Jesus to heal him. Jesus did—he did something to the man and then the man could hear and speak.

What did Jesus do? Follow the numbers in the dot-to-dot to make a picture. Then write the letters, in order, on the lines below.

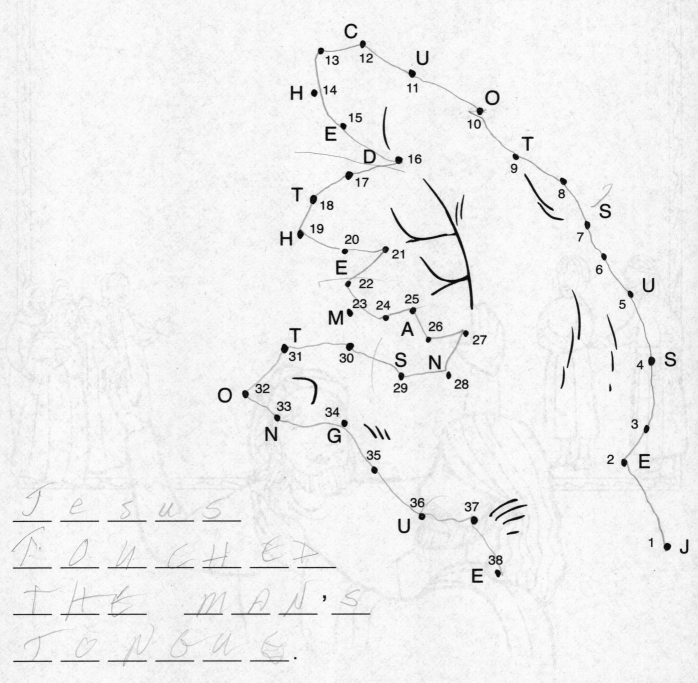

J E S U S

T O U C H E D

T H E   M A N ' S

T O N G U E .

Jesus, My Helper

Jesus helped a man who couldn't see by healing him. Jesus helps you too!
Write or draw a way Jesus helps you.

Who Said It?

Jesus healed a man who said, "Lord, I believe in you!" Write the first letter of each picture to find out whom Jesus healed.

$$\underset{1}{\underline{B}} \; \underset{2}{\underline{L}} \; \underset{3}{\underline{I}} \; \underset{4}{\underline{N}} \; \underset{5}{\underline{D}} \qquad \underset{6}{\underline{M}} \; \underset{7}{\underline{A}} \; \underset{8}{\underline{N}}$$

Helping Others

Jesus told a story about a man helping an injured man whom no one else would help. Use the code to find out where the helper was from.

1=A	2=M	3=S	4=R	5=I

S A M A R I A
3 1 2 1 4 5 1

Maze to Jericho

Jesus told a story to teach us how to love our neighbors. Help the good man from Samaria take the hurt man to an inn to rest and get well.

Mary and Martha

Color this picture of Mary and Martha listening to Jesus teach about God.

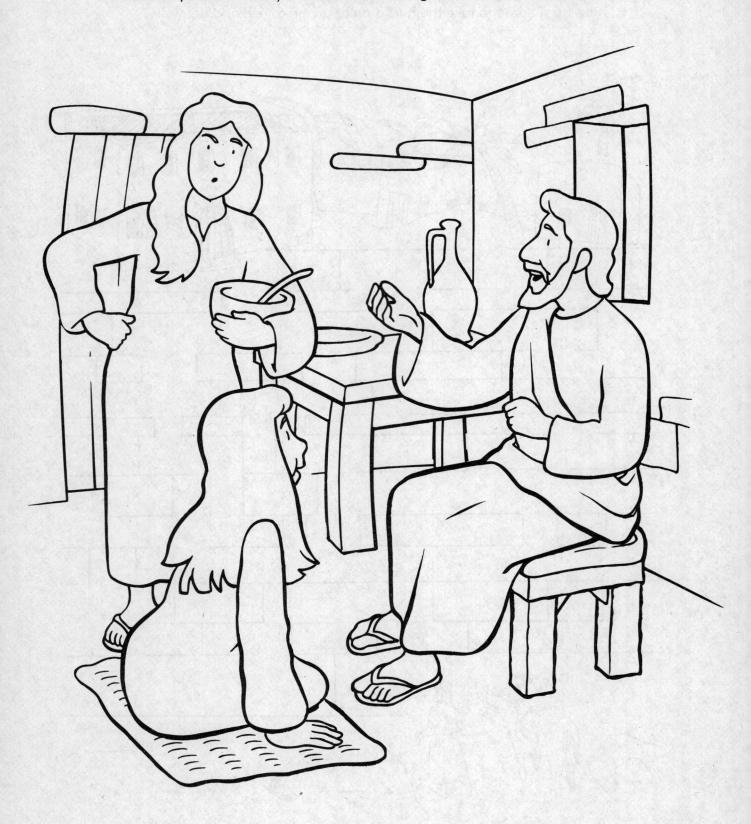

Disciple Match-Up

Jesus taught his disciples to pray. Find the two praying disciples who are the same.

Connect the Numbers

Jesus told a story about a father who gave a party for his son. Connect the matching numbers to find the reason why.

The Lost Sheep

Help the shepherd find his lost sheep.

Word Scramble

In Bethany, Jesus brought Lazarus back to life. Unscramble the words to see what Jesus said.

_ _ _ _ _ _ _ ,

_ _ _ _   _ _ _ !

Only One Came Back

Jesus healed ten men, but only one came back to thank him. Help the man find his way to Jesus. Then read the story in Luke 17:11-19.

START

FINISH

Hidden Word

On the road to Samaria, Jesus healed ten men. Only one man gave praise to God. What did the man say to Jesus? Color the spaces with the dots.

Hidden Message

Color all the balloons that have lowercase letters. Write the uppercase letters in order on the lines below. The message will remind you of something one man in the Bible did and something you should do.

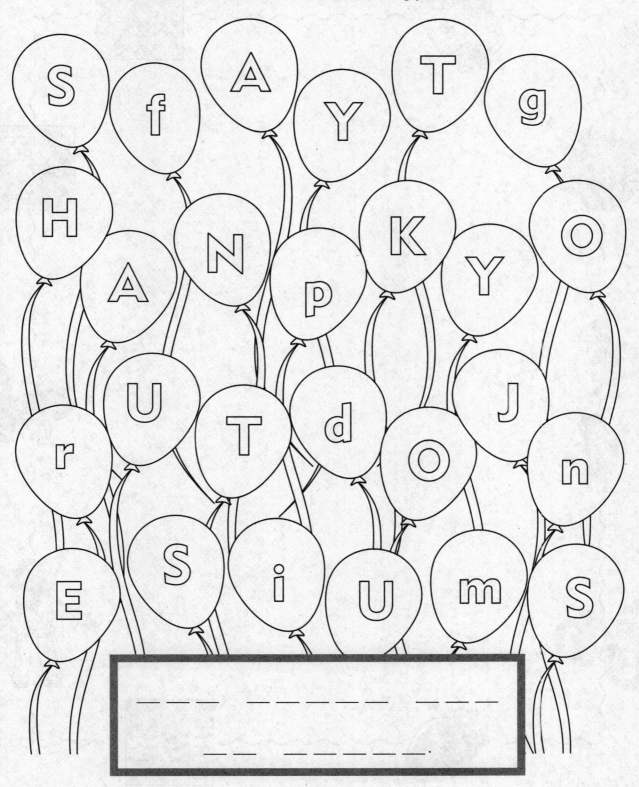

Thank You, Jesus

Draw pictures of some things you would like to thank Jesus for.

Jesus and the Children

Color this picture of Jesus welcoming the children.

Maze

Jesus said, "Let the children come to me." Help the children find their way to Jesus.

FINISH

START

Jesus and You

Jesus welcomed the children and loved them. Jesus loves you too! Trace the letters and connect the dots for a special message you can give to Jesus.

Use the Code

Write the first letter of each picture on the line. What is the secret message?

___ ___ ___ ___ ___

___ ___   ___ ___

_____ .

A Special Message

The same special message is written in five different languages on this page. Solve the puzzle to find out the special message in English. Write the letters in the shapes on the correct blanks. Practice saying the message in all of the languages.

Jesus lo ama.   Italian

Jésus m'aime.   French

Jésus me ama.   Spanish

Jesus liebt mich.   German

Jesus ama-me.   Portuguese

English

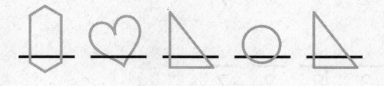

Heart Code

Jesus held the boys and girls and blessed them. Use the code to find out how Jesus feels about you.

S = 7

U = 6

J = 5

L = 4

V = 8

E = 2

O = 3

Y = 1

$$\overline{}_{5} \ \overline{}_{2} \ \overline{}_{7} \ \overline{}_{6} \ \overline{}_{7}$$

$$\overline{}_{4} \ \overline{}_{3} \ \overline{}_{8} \ \overline{}_{2} \ \overline{}_{7}$$

$$\overline{}_{1} \ \overline{}_{3} \ \overline{}_{6} \ .$$

Connect the Dots

Zacchaeus climbed up high to see Jesus when Jesus came to Jericho.
What did Zacchaeus climb?

Zacchaeus and Jesus

How did Zacchaeus see over the crowd when Jesus came? Connect the dots to find out.

Color and Find

Mary of Bethany poured expensive perfume on Jesus' feet. Color the spaces with dots to see what the perfume was carried in.

Color by Number

A crowd greeted Jesus as he entered Jerusalem on a donkey colt.

1=BROWN   2=GREEN   3=WHITE   4=BLUE

Maze

Jesus rode into Jerusalem on a donkey colt. Help the donkey colt take Jesus through the city.

Praise Jesus!

People shouted praises to Jesus when he rode into Jerusalem. Pretend that you were there. What would you have shouted? Use the Word Bank to finish the puzzle.

Word Bank

- JESUS
- KING
- LORD
- SAVIOR
- SON OF GOD

Son of God

King

Hosanna!

If Jesus walked down your street today, what would you do or say to praise him?

Jesus, you help me

Thank you, Jesus, for

Jesus, I think you're really

Jesus, one of the greatest things about you is

Jesus Washes Feet

The words in the basin will help you remember the time Jesus washed his disciples' feet. See if you can find the words in the basin on the towel. Look up, down, across, backwards, and diagonally.

Peter   Towel   Hands
Water   Disciples   Feet
Basin   Others   Jesus
Head   Supper

D M I P H S O H O D
O I E H U V T E Y L
T E S P F S H A T I
T L P C L O E D L T
X E L F I I R R T R
R K M G G P S S E L
N I S A B S L T I E
T F H D N J E E M W
F W H E R P E H S O
W A T E R A I S A T
U L H J G Q H G U C
O F E E T B Y R L S
L I C Q Y V V W A O
W L O S D N A H D T

Remember Jesus

Jesus ate the Passover meal with his followers just before he died. He took two things from the table and told the followers that these two things would forever be used to remember his death. What were these two things? To find out, complete the two dot-to-dots. You can read about these two things in Matthew 26:17-30.

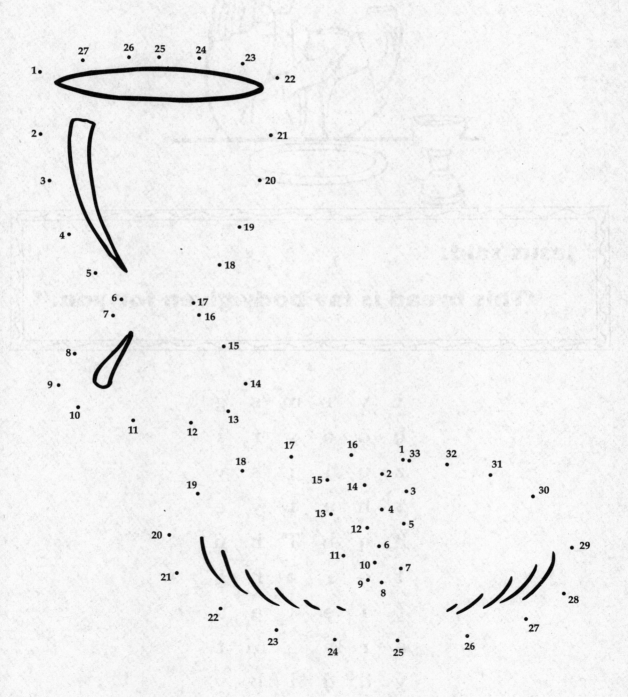

Remember This!

Read what Jesus said. Then find and circle Jesus' words in the word search below.

Jesus said:

"This bread is my body given for you."

```
i  y  r  m  s  g
b  o  d  y  r  i
z  u  l  i  s  v
t  h  a  t  y  e
b  q  b  T  h  n
f  o  r  h  h  g
t  i  e  i  a  a
a  r  a  s  m  t
y  d  d  l  b  v
```

Jesus' Last Supper

This is a picture of Jesus and his friends at the last supper. There are ten things wrong with this picture. Circle them as you find them.

Word Search

Jesus asked his friends to remember him in a special way. Find the words.
Look up, across, and down.

Word Bank

- BREAD
- MEAL
- JESUS
- FRIENDS
- CUP

```
A  F  G  K  U  L  M
J  E  S  U  S  Z  E
B  L  D  A  N  Q  A
I  B  Q  B  R  E  L
F  R  I  E  N  D  S
A  E  Q  U  Q  Z  P
D  A  Z  P  Y  X  U
V  D  Y  I  P  O  C
B  A  V  T  Q  Y  X
```

Which One?

While Jesus prayed in a place called Gethsemane, his friends fell asleep.
Which path leads back to where they are sleeping?

Jesus' Death

More than one person was a part of Jesus' death. Find out about some of them.

1. Who wanted to have Jesus killed?

   Color all the shapes with **1** in them the same color.

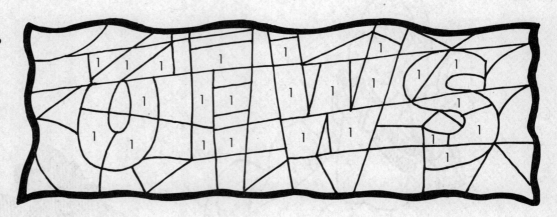

2. Who gave Jesus to the Jews to be killed?

   Color all the shapes with **2** in them the same color.

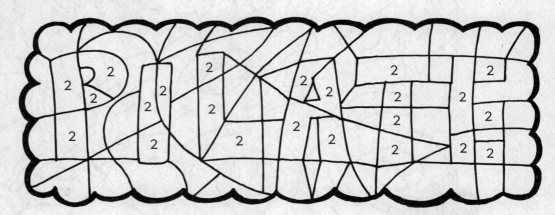

3. Who put Jesus on the cross?

   Color all the shapes with **3** in them the same color.

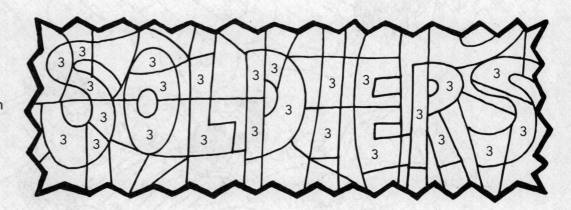

Jesus Dies But Is Alive!

Use the Word Bank and picture clues to finish the puzzle. Read Matthew 28 to find out more about Jesus' death and resurrection.

Word Bank

- ANGEL
- CROSS
- JESUS
- TOMB
- WOMAN

Hidden Word

Color the blocks to see what God can do about our sins because of Jesus.

1=YELLOW   2=BLUE   3=RED   4=GREEN

Number Code

After Jesus was buried in a tomb, something covered the opening of the tomb. Use the number code to find out what it was. Then color the picture.

1=N 2=T 3=S 4=E 5=O

___ ___ ___ ___ ___
 3   2   5   1   4

Picture Search

Jesus' tomb was empty! Angels rolled away the stone. Jesus is alive! Find these pictures in the puzzle in the same order as below. Look up, across, and down.

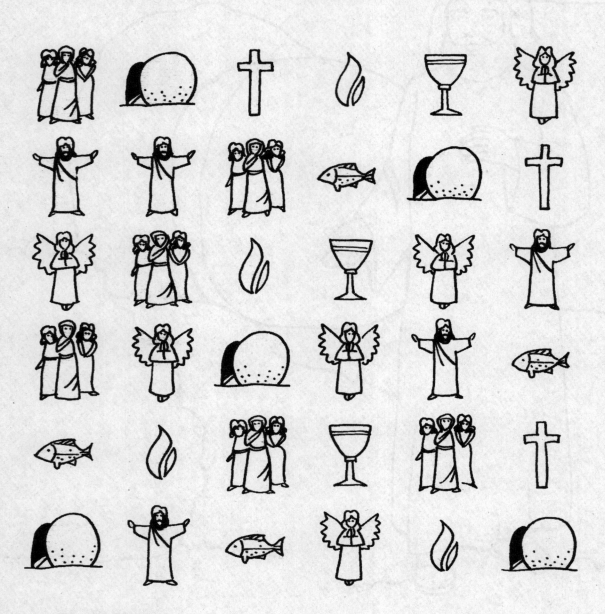

Jesus Is Alive!

Color this picture of the women finding an angel at the empty tomb of Jesus.

Angel Match-Up

Two angels told the women that Jesus had risen from the dead. Find the angels that are alike.

Spell It

The women at the tomb were surprised that Jesus' tomb was empty. Color every square with *J, O,* or *Y.* Then unscramble the letters to find who else was there.

J	O	Y	O	J	S
O	J	G	Y	O	J
Y	O	J	O	Y	O
A	Y	O	E	O	Y
J	O	Y	O	J	O
O	J	O	Y	L	J
Y	N	J	O	Y	O

Maze

Mary ran to tell Peter and John that Jesus' tomb was empty. Help Mary find the disciples.

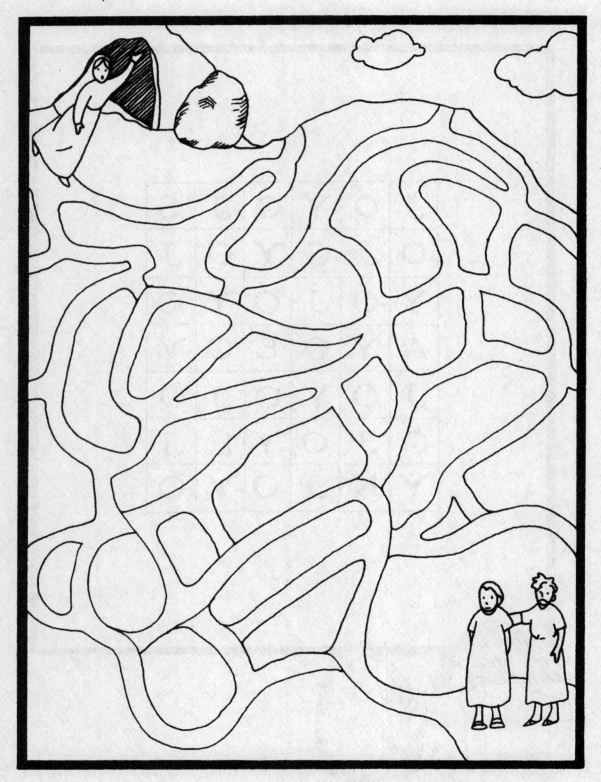

Color It!

Color these words to help you remember that Jesus is alive!

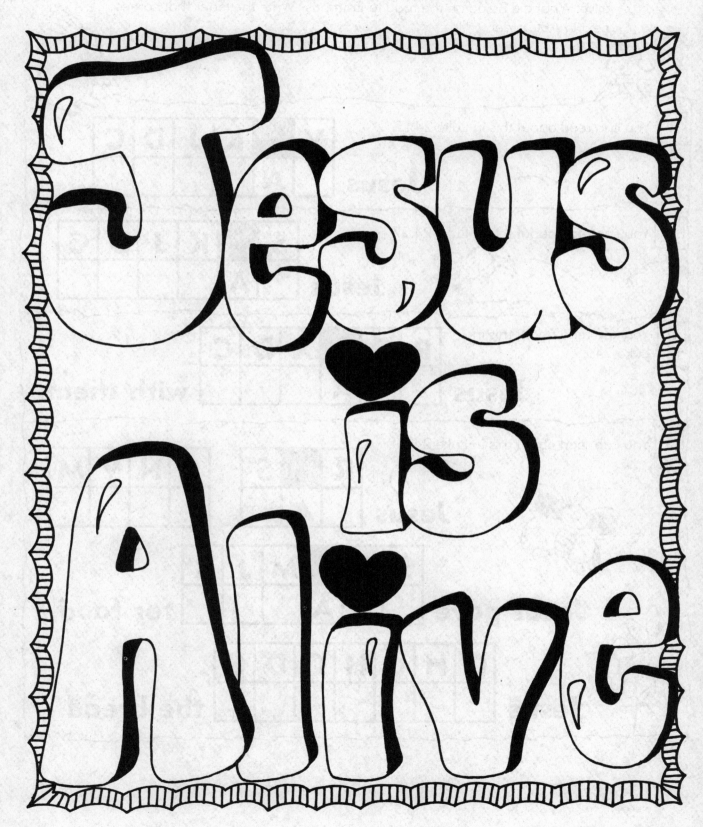

The Road to Emmaus

Jesus did many things after he rose from the dead to show he was really alive. What did he do on the road to Emmaus? Write the letter that comes next in ABC order.

1 You can read about this in Luke 24:15.

V		K	J	D	C

Jesus [| A | | |].

2 You can read about this in Luke 24:27.

S		K	J	D	C

Jesus [| A | | |].

3 You can read about this in Luke 24:29.

R	S		X	D	C

Jesus [| | A | | |] with them.

4 You can read about this in Luke 24:30.

R		S		C	N	V	M

Jesus [| A |] [| | |].

S	G		M	J	R

Jesus gave [| | A | | |] for food.

C	H	U	H	C	D	C

Jesus [| | | | | | |] the bread.

Connect the Dots

What did Jesus cook for his friends? Connect both sets of dots to find out.

Picture Code

The disciples saw Jesus go up into _____. Write the first letter of each picture to complete the sentence.

___ ___ ___ ___ ___ ___
1 2 3 4 5 6

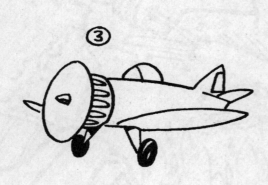

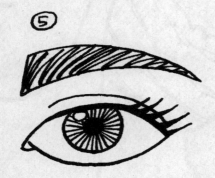

Picture Search

The disciples praised God after Jesus went back to Heaven. Find these pictures in the box in the same order as below. Look up, down, and across.

Peter Preaches

Use the number code to find out whom Peter preached about.

1=S   2=E   3=J   4=U

$\frac{}{3}$ $\frac{}{2}$ $\frac{}{1}$ $\frac{}{4}$ $\frac{}{1}$

What Day Was It?

The Holy Spirit came on the disciples with the sound of a mighty wind and what looked like tongues of fire. What was the Jewish holiday when this happened? Use the code to find the answer.

___ ___ ___ ___ ___ ___ ___ ___ ___
4   1   6   7   1   2   5   3   7

A Happy Man

In the name of Jesus, Peter healed a man who could not walk. How many outlines of the happy man do you see?

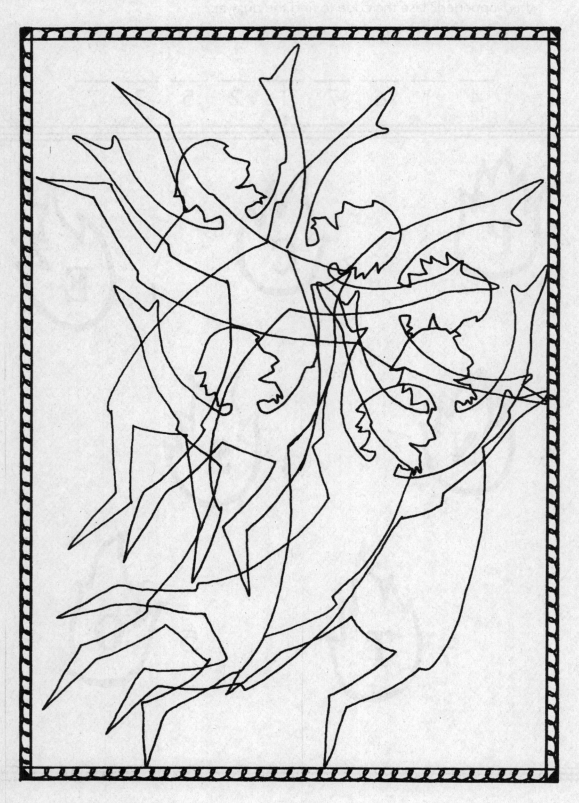

Picture Search

Peter told the people that the power of Jesus had healed the man. Find these figures in the same order as below. Look up, down, and across.

Philip Tells About Jesus

Color this picture of Philip telling a man from Ethiopia about Jesus.

Color by Number

On the road to Damascus, Paul saw a bright light and heard Jesus speak to him. Color the picture.

1=BROWN	3=GREEN	5=YELLOW
2=PURPLE	4=BLUE	

Saul's Conversion

Paul was called Saul before he followed Jesus. While Saul was on his way to Damascus, a light from Heaven blinded him. Use the braille chart to decode the missing words. (See Acts 9:1-19.)

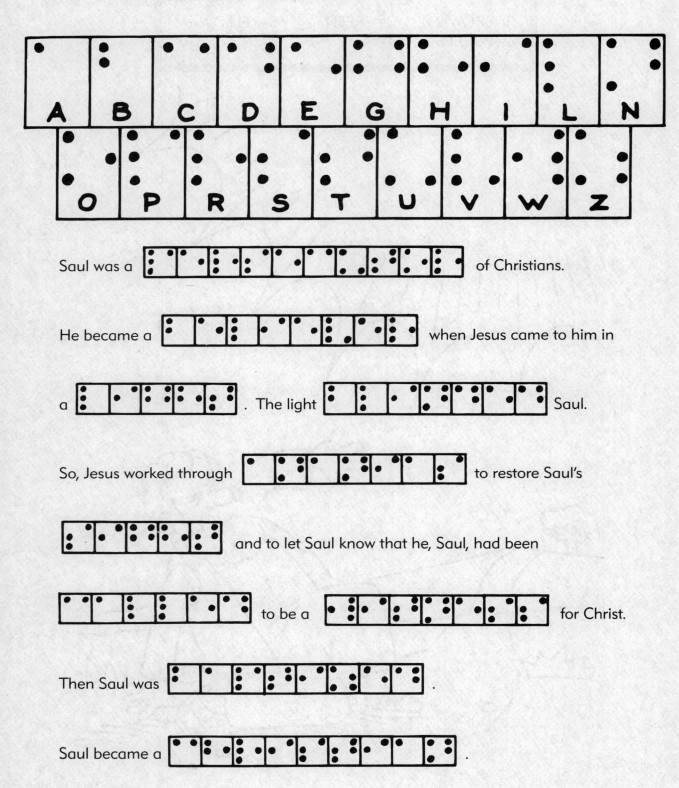

Saul was a ☐☐☐☐☐☐☐☐☐ of Christians.

He became a ☐☐☐☐☐☐☐ when Jesus came to him in

a ☐☐☐☐☐ . The light ☐☐☐☐☐☐☐ Saul.

So, Jesus worked through ☐☐☐☐☐ to restore Saul's

☐☐☐☐☐ and to let Saul know that he, Saul, had been

☐☐☐☐☐ to be a ☐☐☐☐☐☐☐ for Christ.

Then Saul was ☐☐☐☐☐☐☐ .

Saul became a ☐☐☐☐☐☐☐☐ .

Saul Learns About Jesus

Finish this picture. Draw Saul falling to the ground as the light from Heaven came.

Connect the Dots

After he believed in Jesus, people wanted to kill Paul. How did Paul escape from Damascus?

Dorcas Is a Helper

What did Dorcas make to give to people? Connect the dots to find out.

Maze

Help Barnabas find Paul in Tarsus, then take them to the city of Antioch.

Where's Paul?

Many people in the places Paul visited became believers in Jesus. Can you find Paul in the crowd?

Paul's Travels

Paul was a great missionary who traveled to many places. Help Paul's boat get across the sea so he can visit the people on the other side to tell them about Jesus.

Number Code

In the city of Antioch, Paul preached in the _____. Use the number code to discover the name of this place.

1=S 2=E 3=Y 4=U 5=N 6=G 7=A 8=O

__ __ __ __ __ __ __ __ __
1 3 5 7 6 8 6 4 2

Paul and Barnabas

Circle the words from the Bible story in Acts 14 that are hidden in the puzzle. Use the Word Bank to help you.

Word Bank

- PAUL
- BARNABAS
- MAN
- WALK
- HEAL
- TEACH

```
D Y B P M F H L
G N A U A M E O
T Q R K N V A B
E S N P J B L Q
A M A F R Z X I
C G B H W A L K
H P A U L X S V
J W S E N H R C
```

Word Search

In Lystra, people thought Paul and Barnabas were the Greek gods Zeus and Hermes. Find these names in the puzzle. Look up, across, and down.

Word Bank
- LYSTRA
- ZEUS
- PAUL
- HERMES
- BARNABAS

```
A  L  Y  S  T  R  A
V  M  U  W  A  O  B
M  R  F  D  S  Y  A
P  Q  O  W  I  E  R
F  L  S  K  A  J  N
S  P  A  U  L  I  A
U  B  H  B  J  M  B
E  Z  W  X  E  C  A
Z  H  E  R  M  E  S
```

Timothy Match-Up

In Lystra, Timothy joined Paul on his travels to tell others about Jesus. Find the two pictures of Timothy that are alike.

What Was It?

Write the first letter of each picture to find out what kind of cloth Lydia sold.

$\overline{}$ $\overline{}$ $\overline{}$ $\overline{}$ $\overline{}$ $\overline{}$
 1   2   3   4   5   6

Lydia Follows Jesus

Color this picture of Lydia. Paul and Silas helped her learn about Jesus.

Paul and Silas in Jail

Acts 16:16-34 tells that Paul and Silas were beaten by the Roman officers and thrown into jail. Instead of complaining, Paul and Silas did something very strange.

Color in all the solid bars of the jail. Don't color the bars with broken lines. When you are finished, you'll see what Paul and Silas did.

What Time Was It?

In Philippi, Paul and Silas went to jail for telling people about Jesus. What time was it when they were praying and singing and God sent an earthquake to rescue them?

____ ____ ____ ____ ____ ____ ____ ____
  4   2   5   6   2   7   3   1

Use the Code

Paul and Silas were put in prison for preaching about Jesus. God rescued them with an _____. Use the code to find the answer.

__ __ __ __ __ __ __ __ __ __
1 2 3 4 5 6 7 2 8 1

Connect the Dots

In Berea, the people who heard Paul preach checked the Scriptures to see if Paul was telling the truth. What were the Scriptures written on?

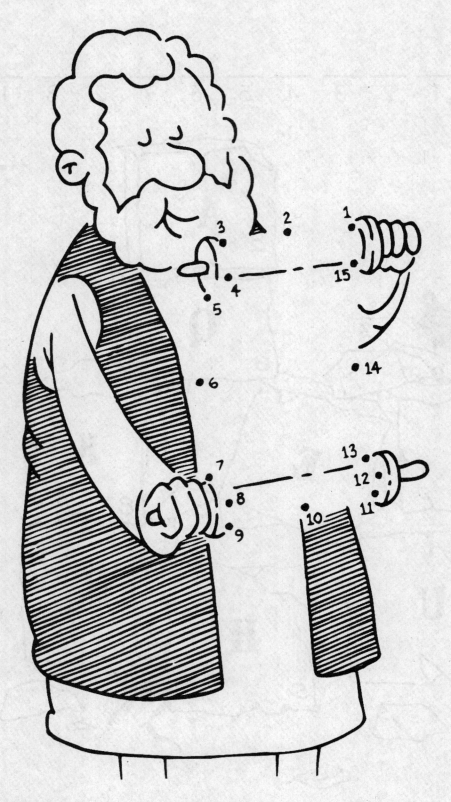

Marketplace Mix-Up

In Athens, Paul met with people in the marketplace and told them about Jesus. Find six things wrong with this picture.

Finish the Picture

In Corinth, Paul worked as a tentmaker. Finish the tent.

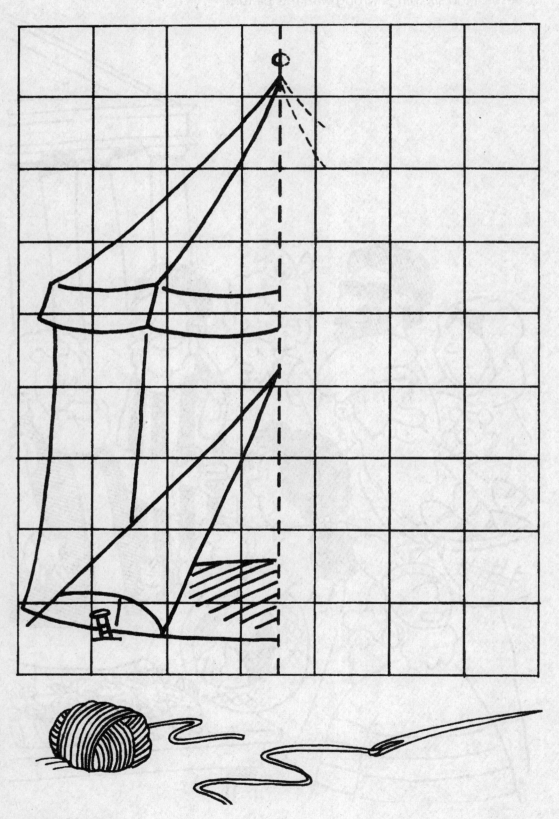

Paul Worked Hard

What did Paul make? Connect the dots to find out.

Color by Number

Use the code to color the picture.

In the city of Troas, a young man listening to Paul went to sleep and fell out the window.

1=BLUE
2=GREEN
3=GRAY
4=BROWN
5=YELLOW

Paul Tells About Jesus

Finish this picture by drawing the crowd of people who were listening to Paul tell about Jesus.

Word Search

On the way to Rome, Paul was shipwrecked on an island called Malta. Find these words in the puzzle. Look up, across, and down.

• ROME   • PAUL   • MALTA   • ISLAND

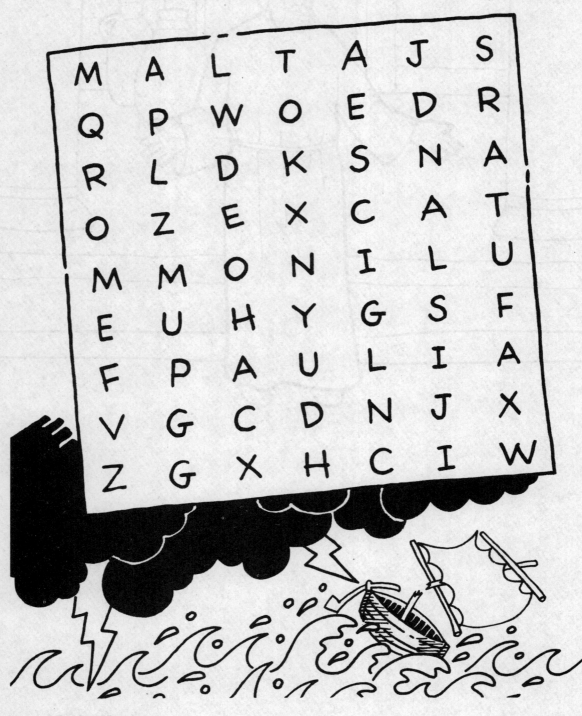

Paul Is Shipwrecked

Color this picture of Paul and the others who were shipwrecked on the island of Malta.

Word Wheel

For two years in Rome, Paul lived in his own rented _____. Write the first letter of each picture to finish the sentence.

__ __ __ __ __
1 2 3 4 5

Priscilla and Aquila

Where did Priscilla and Aquila's church meet? Connect the dots to find out.

Mixed Fruit

The fruit below is mixed up. Write the letters from the apples on the first set of blanks below to find one fruit of the Spirit. Then do the same for the oranges, lemons, bananas, pineapples, strawberries, grapes, raspberries, and pears. The first fruit shown is an apple, the second is an orange, the third is a lemon, and so on, to help you know which fruit is which. Read Galatians 5:22, 23.

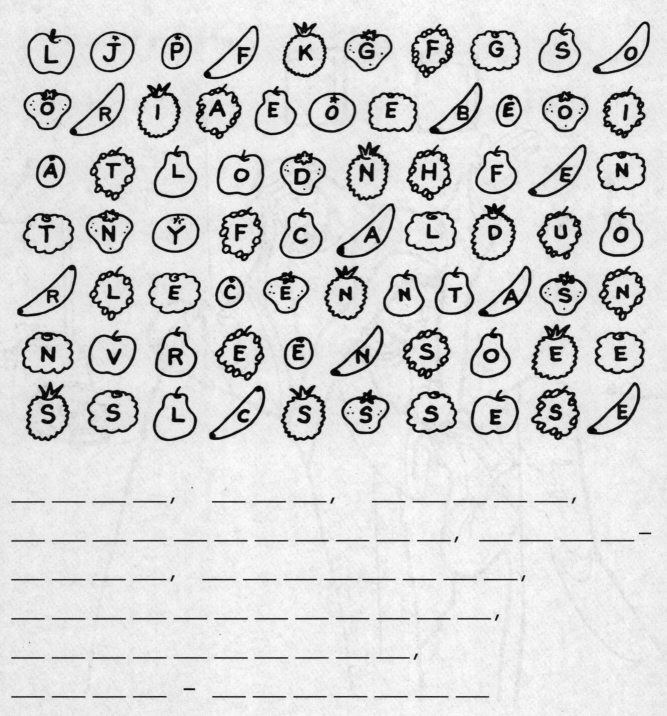

_____ _____ _____ _____ _____ _____ , _____ _____ _____ _____ _____ , _____ _____ _____ _____ _____ ,

_____ _____ _____ _____ _____ _____ _____ _____ _____ _____ _____ , _____ _____ _____ _____ _____

_____ _____ _____ _____ _____ , _____ _____ _____ _____ _____ _____ _____ ,

_____ _____ _____ _____ _____ _____ _____ _____ _____ _____ _____ ,

_____ _____ _____ _____ _____ _____ _____ _____ _____ _____ ,

_____ _____ _____ _____ — _____ _____ _____ _____ _____

Learning About Jesus

What did Timothy read to learn about Jesus? Connect the dots to find out.

Word Search

Timothy's grandmother, Lois, and his mother, Eunice, taught him about God. Find these names in the puzzle. Look up, across, and down.

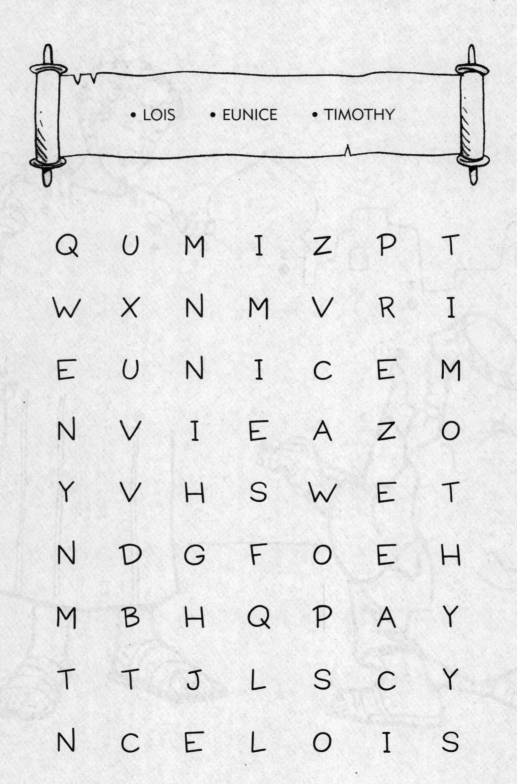

• LOIS   • EUNICE   • TIMOTHY

Q U M I Z P T

W X N M V R I

E U N I C E M

N V I E A Z O

Y V H S W E T

N D G F O E H

M B H Q P A Y

T T J L S C Y

N C E L O I S

Run the Race

Do you like races? Do you like to watch them or do you like to participate? There are different kinds of races: track, swimming, car, and many more. Follow the maze to find out what Paul says about racing in Hebrews 12:1.

"Let us RUN THE RACE marked out for us."

Heaven Will Be . . .

Place a pencil inside the dotted lines to help you finish the sentences that tell something about Heaven. To find out more, read Revelation 21 and 22.

God will wipe away all ____.

"I am the Beginning and the ____."

There will be no more ____.

There is no ____ there.

Everything will be ____.

"I am coming ____."

Heavenly Praise

The last book of the Bible, Revelation, tells how God is praised in Heaven. In the puzzle below, fifteen words relating to the praise of God are hidden. See if you can find them all!

Word Bank

- ANGEL
- BLESSED
- GLORY
- GOD
- HEAR
- HONOR
- JESUS
- LANGUAGE
- PEOPLE
- POWER
- PRAISE
- STRENGTH
- THANKS
- THRONE
- WISDOM

```
B W M J B H E A R H Q D T
P I O A L O N G L N O E H
G S V C E F P R A I S E A
T D U K S T R E N G T H N
H O J E S U S R G R Y L K
R M B S E A N E U T J D S
O X G O D R L W A N G E L
N E W N K I Z O G L O R Y
E H O N O R C P E O P L E
```

I Think Heaven Will . . .

What do you think Heaven will look like? What will you see? Who will be there? Draw a picture of your "heavenly" ideas in the frame below.

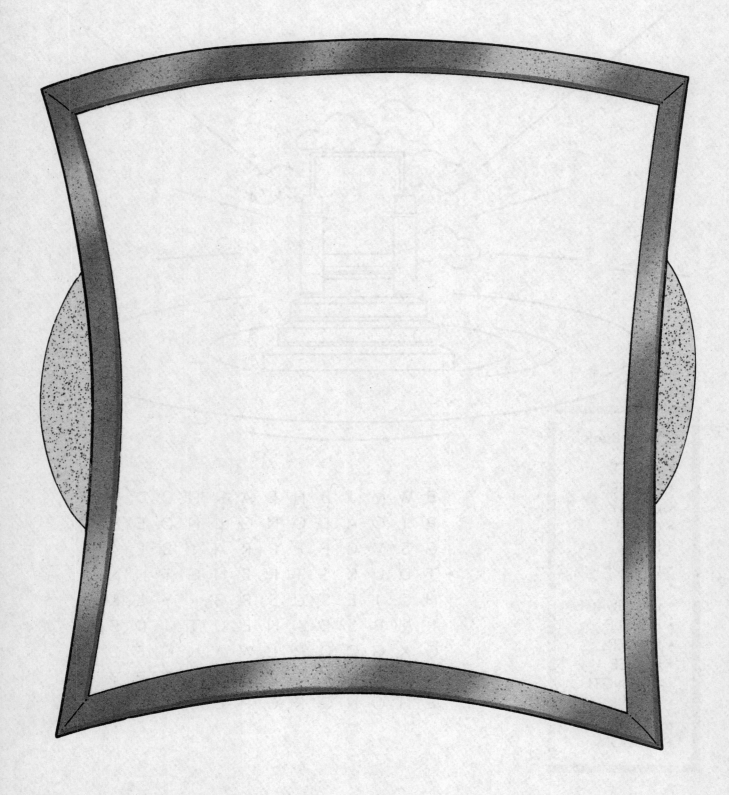

Color by Number

Jesus is coming soon! Use the code to color the picture.

1=BLUE	3=WHITE	5=BROWN
2=PURPLE	4=PINK	6=YELLOW

Bible Riddle #1

What appears once in the Old Testament, two times in the New Testament, yet is not in the Bible? To answer the riddle, color in each space that contains a dot.

Bible Riddle #2

Why is the Bible like a modern skyscraper? To answer the riddle, begin at the arrow and follow the path from START to FINISH. When you come to each letter, write it in a circle below the path.

START

FINISH

Answers

Page 3
sky and earth

Page 4

Page 7
stars

Page 10

Page 11

Page 12

Page 13
birds have wings, turtles have shells, elephants have trunks, giraffes have long necks, camels have humps, fish have fins

Page 14

Page 15

Page 18
Day 1, picture 4; Day 2, picture 5; Day 3, picture 3; Day 4, picture 2; Day 5, picture 1; Day 6, picture 6

Page 19

Page 22

Page 23

Page 24

Page 25

None of these creatures was the right helper for Adam.

Page 26

Page 27

Page 28

Page 29

Page 30

Just before Eve

Page 31

It didn't have a leg to stand on.

Page 32

They raised Cain.

Page 34

God saved Noah.

Page 35

Page 36

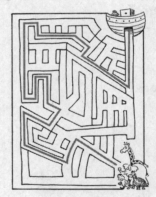

Page 38

No, the worms came in apples.

Page 39

forty days

Page 40

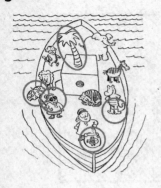

Page 41

Page 43

Page 44

Page 45

Page 46
flood lamps

Page 47

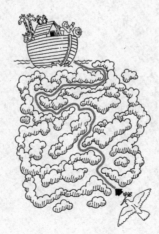

Page 50

Page 51

Page 52

Page 53
Is anything too hard for God?

Page 54

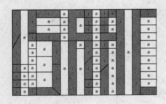

Page 55

Page 57
wells of water

Page 58

Page 61

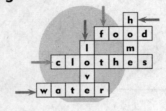

Page 63

```
    J
C O A T
  S
  E
D R E A M E R
  P
  H
```

Page 65
Pharaoh

Page 66
for good measure

Page 67

Page 68
He did his best.

Page 71
basket

Page 72

Page 73
Moses; to pull out

Page 74

Page 75

Page 76

Page 77

Page 78

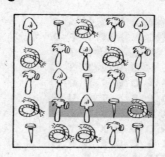

Page 81

Page 82

Bring my people out of Egypt.

Page 83

Page 84

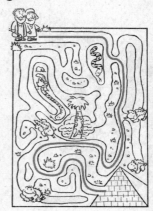

Page 85

Page 86

Page 87

Page 95

Page 101

Page 88

Page 96

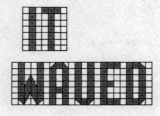

Page 97

It stayed parted for a short time.

Page 102

Page 90

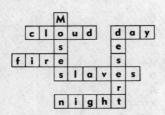

Page 91

Red Sea

Page 92

Do not be afraid.

Page 99

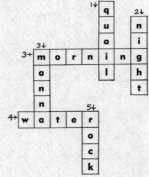

Page 100

five

Page 103

370   Answers

Page 106

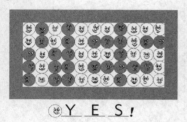

Page 107

one hundred and twenty

Page 108

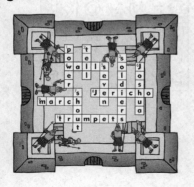

☺ Y E S !

Page 109

Be strong. Have courage. I will be with you. I will not leave you.

Page 110

on Rahab's roof

Page 111

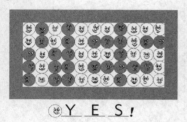

Page 113

Page 115

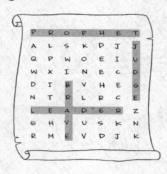

Page 117

Page 118

Samson—because he brought down the house

Page 119

Page 121

friend

Page 122

bread

Page 124

Samuel listened to God and obeyed.

Page 126

Page 127

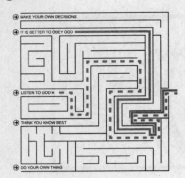

Page 128

Page 131

Page 132

Page 134

Page 135

king

Page 136

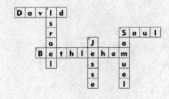

Page 137

— You need to get back to tending your sheep.

— Goliath is over 9 feet tall.

— You are just a boy.

+ You have killed a lion and a bear by yourself.

+ No one else will fight Goliath.

— Goliath has a full suit of armor.

— Saul's armor is too big for you.

— All you have is a sling.

— You could be killed.

+ There is a great reward for defeating Goliath.

+ Goliath has openly spoken against God.

+ You have God on your side.

Page 138

He gave it his best shot.

Page 139

Page 140

Page 141

Page 144

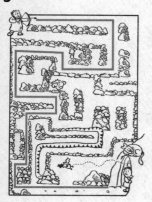

Page 145

Page 147

Page 148

temple

Page 149

Page 151

ravens

Page 153

"Let each one go home in peace."

Page 154

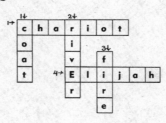

Page 156

1. Hezekiah, prophet; 2. wall, prayed; 4. Isaiah; 5. prayer; 8. sign; 10. steps; The Lord will do what he says.

Page 158

king

Page 160

As long as he sought the Lord, God gave him success.

Page 161

Page 162

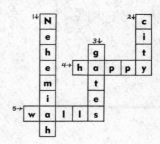

Page 164

Page 166

Page 167

Page 168

Job. Because he had a lot of patience.

Page 169

Psalms

Page 170

Page 171

The Lord; 1. pastures, 2. nothing, 3. green, 4. leads, 5. soul, 6. waters, 7. goodness

Page 172

six

Page 173

Page 174

Here am I. Send me.

Page 175

Wonderful Counselor

Page 176

eagle

Page 178

Page 179

Page 180

No other god can save in this way!

Page 184

angel

Page 185

Page 186

ten before one

Page 187

Page 189

like he was in way over his head

Page 190

Page 191

Bethlehem

Page 192

Page 193

Page 194

Immanuel

Page 196

God's Son, Jesus

Page 197

Page 198

Page 199

Page 200

Page 202

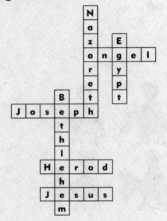

Page 203

Page 205
six

Page 207

Page 208
Today in the town of David a Savior has been born to you; he is Christ the Lord.

Page 210
glory to God

Page 212

Page 213
five

Page 214

Page 215

Page 216

Page 220

Page 222

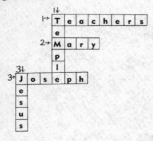

Page 223

Page 224

Page 226

his father's house

Page 227

Page 229

Stop doing wrong. Start doing right.

Page 230

Page 231

desert, locusts, honey, voice, Pharisees, sin, forgave, Son

Page 232

Page 233

dove

Page 234

I love you. I am very pleased with you.

Page 235

Page 237

Go away from me, Satan! It is written in the Scriptures, "You must worship the Lord your God. Serve only him!"

Page 238

ten

Page 239

Nicodemus

Page 240

Page 241

"For God so loved the world that he gave his one and only Son."

Page 243

official, Jesus, son, servant, 1, 4, 3, 2

Page 244

Page 245

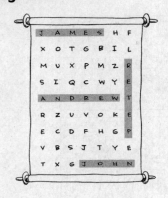

Page 246

followed, boats, partners, Lord, nets, fish; disciples

Page 249

walk, friends, Jesus, hole, well, walked

Page 251

Matthew, follow, everything, feast, friends, complain, lives

Page 253

disciples

Page 254

Page 255

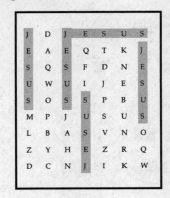

Page 257

Page 258

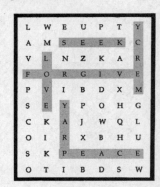

Page 259

Page 260

1. Don't show off. 2. Don't say the same things over and over. 3. Ask God for what you need.

Page 261

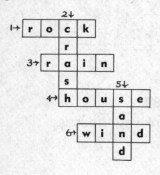

Page 263

forgiveness

Page 264

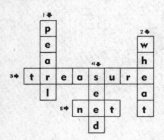

Page 265

Page 266

He commands even the winds and the water, and they obey him.

Page 267

Page 268

How far will they go among so many? They had enough to eat. Twelve baskets of barley loaves were left over.

Page 269

Page 270

Page 271

Page 272

Page 274

Page 275
Jesus touched the man's tongue.

Page 277
blind man

Page 278
Samaria

Page 279

Page 281

Page 282
He's home!

Page 283

Page 284
Lazarus, come out!

Page 285

Page 286

Page 287
Say thank you to Jesus.

Page 290

Page 292
Jesus is my friend.

Page 293
Jesus loves me!

Page 294
Jesus loves you.

Page 297

Page 299

Page 300

Page 302

Page 304

Page 305

Page 306

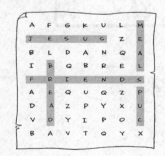

Page 307

Page 308

Page 309

Page 310

Page 311
stone

Page 312

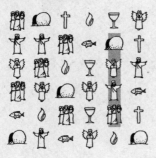

Page 314

Page 315
angels

Page 316

Page 318
1. Jesus walked. 2. Jesus talked.
3. Jesus stayed with them.
4. Jesus sat down. Jesus gave
thanks for food. Jesus divided
the bread.

Page 319
fish and bread

Page 320
Heaven

Page 321

Page 322
Jesus

Page 323
Pentecost

Page 324
six

Page 325

Page 328
persecutor, believer, light,
blinded, Ananias, sight, called,
witness, baptized, Christian

Page 331
clothes

Page 332

Page 333

Page 334

Page 335

synagogue

Page 336

Page 337

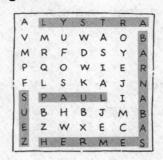

Page 338

Page 339

purple

Page 341

sang praises to God

Page 342

midnight

Page 343

earthquake

Page 344

a scroll

Page 345

Page 347

tents

Page 350

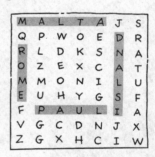

Page 352

house

Page 353

their home

Page 354

love, joy, peace, forbearance, kindness, goodness, faithfulness, gentleness, self-control

Page 355

God's Word

Page 356

Page 357

Page 358

tears, end, death, night, new, soon

Page 359

Page 362

Page 363

It contains many beautiful stories.